LIVING STONES

ROCKS

SUSAN SAYERS

Illustrated by
Fred Chevalier

Kevin
Mayhew

First published in 1999 by
KEVIN MAYHEW LTD
Buxhall
Stowmarket
Suffolk IP14 3BW

0 1 2 3 4 5 6 7 8 9

ISBN 1 84003 398 3
Catalogue No. 1500292

The other titles in the *Living Stones* series are		
Complete Resource Book	ISBN 1 84003 396 7	Cat. No. 1500290
Prayers of Intercession	ISBN 1 84003 395 9	Cat. No. 1500294
Pebbles	ISBN 1 84003 397 5	Cat. No. 1500291
Boulders	ISBN 1 84003 399 1	Cat. No. 1500293

Cover photographs:
Group of children – courtesy of SuperStock Ltd, London
Background – courtesy of Images Colour Library Ltd, London
Cover design by Jaquetta Sergeant
Edited by Katherine Laidler
Typesetting by Louise Selfe
Printed in Great Britain

FOREWORD

For children of primary school age the sense of belonging to a peer group becomes increasingly important. Their faith development can be fostered in group activities which are fun and challenging. Their growing awareness of the wider world is often linked with a strong sense of justice and social responsibility, and they need to see the Christian perspective in all this.

Rocks encourages the children to begin thinking about the implications of their faith. Their participation in the story-telling and teaching is welcomed.

It would be wise to split the group into two age groups, adapting the suggestions on the worksheets accordingly.

This is something of a DIY kit, supplied with plenty of openings to meet your own parish needs and the needs of the children, and to spark off your own imaginative ideas. It is based on the belief that children are as much a part of the Church as adults, and that there is great value in sharing the same teaching each Sunday whatever our age. This book follows the weekly readings of the Common Worship Lectionary (Principal Service) for Year B of the three-year cycle, so that the whole church will have that common experience.

Rocks includes a series of weekly activity sheets. These may be copied without further permission or charge for non-commercial use. They can be used as they stand, or you can select the material you want. Copy them for the children to take home, use them in church, put them in the magazine or news sheet, distribute them at clubs or Bible study groups, or use them in conjunction with your learning programme. They are 'working sheets' rather than 'work sheets' as they often include instructions for making and doing rather than being complete in themselves. Children will need their leaders to have planned ahead for the resources needed.

When planning for children's work it is advisable to read through the Bible passages prayerfully. You are then in a better position to see how the programme relates to the readings, and also to supplement and vary the programme as a result of your own insights and the specific needs of your group.

The children are encouraged to pray during the week, using the suggestions on their sheet. These can be built into a collection of prayers and made into a personal prayer book.

A few general ideas about story-telling:

- Tell the story from the viewpoint of a character in the situation. To create the time-machine effect, avoid eye contact as you slowly put on the appropriate cloth or cloak, and then make eye contact as you greet the children in character.

- Have an object with you which leads into the story – a water jug, or a lunch box, for instance.

- Walk the whole group through the story, so that they are physically moving from one place to another; and use all kinds of places, such as broom cupboards, under the stairs, outside under the trees, and so on.

- Collect some carpet tiles – blue and green – so that at story time the children can sit round the edge of this and help you place on the cut-outs for the story.

You may find it useful to keep a record of what you actually do each week, as well as build up a store of the resources you use, because this will obviously help to make future activities easier to prepare.

It is my hope that this book will not only stimulate ideas and enable a varied programme of children's work to take place, but most of all it will encourage us all, whatever our age, as we make the journey of faith together.

SUSAN SAYERS

ACKNOWLEDGEMENTS

The publishers wish to express their gratitude to the following for permission to reproduce their copyright material in this publication:

CopyCare, PO Box 77, Hailsham, East Sussex, BN27 3EF, for *You are the King of glory,* 1978 Springtide. Used by permission.

Kingsway's Thankyou Music, PO Box 75, Eastbourne, East Sussex, BN23 6NW, UK, for *5000+ Hungry Folk,* 1985. Used by permission.

Make Way Music, P.O. Box 263, Croydon, CR9 5AP, UK, for *My Lord, what love is this* (verse 1 and chorus). All rights reserved. International copyright secured. Used by permission.

CONTENTS

Recommended Bibles   7

ADVENT
    First Sunday of Advent   8
    Second Sunday of Advent   10
    Third Sunday of Advent   12
    Fourth Sunday of Advent   14

CHRISTMAS
    Christmas Day   16
    First Sunday of Christmas   18
    Second Sunday of Christmas   20

EPIPHANY
    The Epiphany   22
    The Baptism of Christ: First Sunday of Epiphany   24
    Second Sunday of Epiphany   26
    Third Sunday of Epiphany   28
    Fourth Sunday of Epiphany   30

ORDINARY TIME
    Proper 1   32
    Proper 2   34
    Proper 3   36
    Second Sunday before Lent   38
    Sunday before Lent   40

LENT
    First Sunday of Lent   42
    Second Sunday of Lent   44
    Third Sunday of Lent   46
    Fourth Sunday of Lent: Mothering Sunday   48
    Fifth Sunday of Lent   50
    Palm Sunday   52

EASTER
    Easter Day   54
    Second Sunday of Easter   56
    Third Sunday of Easter   58
    Fourth Sunday of Easter   60
    Fifth Sunday of Easter   62
    Sixth Sunday of Easter   64
    Ascension Day   66
    Seventh Sunday of Easter   68
    Pentecost   70

ORDINARY TIME

Trinity Sunday	72
Proper 4	74
Proper 5	76
Proper 6	78
Proper 7	80
Proper 8	82
Proper 9	84
Proper 10	86
Proper 11	88
Proper 12	90
Proper 13	92
Proper 14	94
Proper 15	96
Proper 16	98
Proper 17	100
Proper 18	102
Proper 19	104
Proper 20	106
Proper 21	108
Proper 22	110
Proper 23	112
Proper 24	114
Proper 25	116
All Saints' Day	118
Fourth Sunday before Advent	120
Third Sunday before Advent	122
Second Sunday before Advent	124
Christ the King	126
Appendix	129

This book is dedicated to my family and friends,
whose encouraging support has been wonderful,
and to all those whose good ideas are included here for others to share.

RECOMMENDED BIBLES

It is often a good idea to look at a passage in several different versions before deciding which to use for a particular occasion.

As far as children are concerned, separate Bible stories, such as those published by Palm Tree Press and Lion, are a good introduction for the very young. Once children are reading, a very helpful version is the *International Children's Bible* (New Century version) published by Word Publishing. Here children have a translation based on experienced scholarship, using language structure suitable for young readers, with short sentences and appropriate vocabulary. There is a helpful dictionary, and clear maps and pictures are provided.

ADVENT

FIRST SUNDAY OF ADVENT

Thought for the day

Be alert and watchful; keep yourselves ready.

Readings

Isaiah 64:1-9
Psalm 80:1-7, 17-19
1 Corinthians 1:3-9
Mark 13:24-37

Aim

To know that Jesus will be coming back in glory.

Starter

Get ready to . . . Each time the children crouch in the 'get ready' position, and when you show a symbol of a particular activity, they have to mime it until the whistle blows for the 'stop and get ready' stage again. (Possible items might be a football, tennis racket, swimwear and goggles, a horse shoe and a paintbox.)

Teaching

Prepare the signs and symbols below to be placed on the floor during the teaching.

WHERE? **WHEN?** **HOW?** **?**

Explain that Advent means 'coming' and the person we're waiting and preparing for is Jesus. Now place down the '1st' rosette as you tell them about the first time Jesus came to earth. (Involve them and use what they already know.) As you discuss that first coming, place down the picture of the Nativity.

As you display the '2nd' rosette, tell them that the manger at Bethlehem wasn't the only time for Jesus to come to our earth. We are told in the Bible, by the prophets and by Jesus himself, that he will be coming again one day. Place down the 'When?', 'Where?', and 'How?' cards, and read excerpts from today's Gospel to find out the clues we have been given. Go over these in discussion, displaying the big question mark as you draw the clues together and establish that there is still lots we don't know (and even Jesus didn't know) about exact times and dates. What we do know is that it will happen, and we need to make sure we keep ourselves alert, so that we'll be ready for Jesus when he comes in glory.

Praying

Jesus, get us ready to meet you
when you come again in glory,
so that we can welcome you
when we see you face to face.

Activities

During Advent the children will be making a four-stage pop-up model which can eventually be a table centrepiece or a crib at home. Instructions and outlines are given for stage one on this week's worksheet. You may like them to mount the sheet on thin card to make it all stronger. They will need scissors that really work, and colouring materials. Try paints with thin brushes for a change. For younger children you could enlarge the sheets during Advent to A3.

Notes

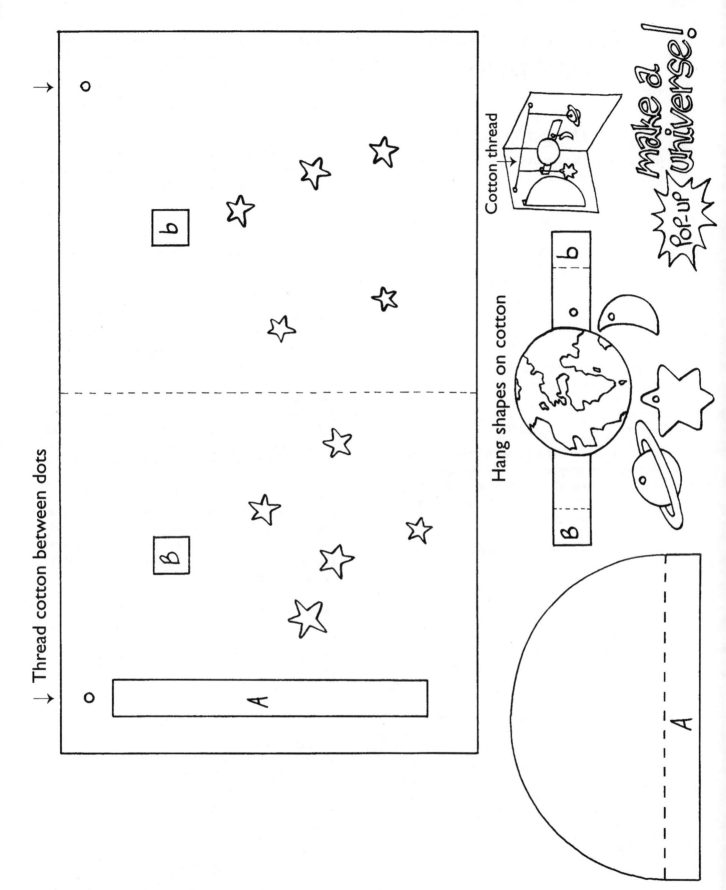

make a Pop-up universe!

Cotton thread

Hang shapes on cotton

Thread cotton between dots

A

B

b

A

B

b

To pray this week

Jesus, get us ready to meet you when you come again in glory, so that we can welcome you when we see you face to face.

SECOND SUNDAY OF ADVENT

Thought for the day

John the Baptist prepares the way for the coming of the Messiah by helping the people to realign their lives.

Readings

Isaiah 40:1-11
Psalm 85:1-2, 8-13
2 Peter 3:8-15a
Mark 1:1-8

Aim

To hear about John the Baptist and his teaching about watching closely.

Starter

What's different? Get into pairs. Take it in turns for one to hide their eyes while the other changes something about the way they are standing or what they are wearing. See if the difference is recognised, then swap roles. Ideas for differences: cross arms in different way, hair tucked behind other ear, shoelace undone/done up, ring on different finger.

Teaching

Sometimes we don't notice things that we are used to seeing. Today we are going to look at someone who got people noticing things they had stopped looking at. (Have two people in conversation for this.)

What was his name?
His name was John. One day no one had heard of him and the next, there he was out in the wild desert outside Jerusalem, drawing huge crowds of people because of what he was saying. They felt he was telling them what they knew they needed to hear. They didn't come because what he said was easy – in fact, it was very challenging – but he made them feel they wanted to go for it with everything they had.

Go for what?
Sorting their lives out. They started to look closely at how they were really thinking and behaving – John helped them notice their own bad habits and the unloving, discontented way they were living. They suddenly wanted to put those things right. John told them it was like road-building.

Road-building?
Yes. He said they needed to build their lives like a good road ready for God to come to them, a road that was straight and true with no mountains of greed or empty pits of cruelty and grumbling. And they needed to start building it straightaway.

Why?
Because John said it wouldn't be very long before God's Messiah was coming to live among them, and they all wanted to be ready for that.

So what did they do about their road-building?
Well, like I said, they had a good look at themselves, saw what needed to be changed, told God about it and then John washed them.

Washed them?
Yes, they waded into the local Jordan river, and when they confessed their sins John dipped them right under the water as a sign that their lives were being washed clean.

That's a good idea. You'd really feel you were making a fresh clean start if you were dipped right under water in a flowing river. Now they would feel they'd done what they could to be ready for the Messiah.
Yes, that's right. And we can do the same, you know.

We can?
Oh, yes. If we take a look at how we speak to people, and what we do for them, and what we don't do for them, we'll soon see which bits of our road need changing. Then we can tell God we've noticed them and are sorry.

What will God do?
He'll forgive us and give us a fresh start.

Perhaps we could do that in the bath or shower?
Good idea.

Praying

Loving God, open my eyes to see
what needs changing and putting right
in my thinking, speaking and doing,
because I want to turn away from sin
and turn towards you.
Amen.

Activities

The children will be making Stage Two of the Christmas pop-up model. There are instructions and outlines for this on the sheet. You may like them to mount it all on thin card for extra strength. As with all the Advent sheets, younger children in ROCKS may find it easier if it is enlarged to A3 size.

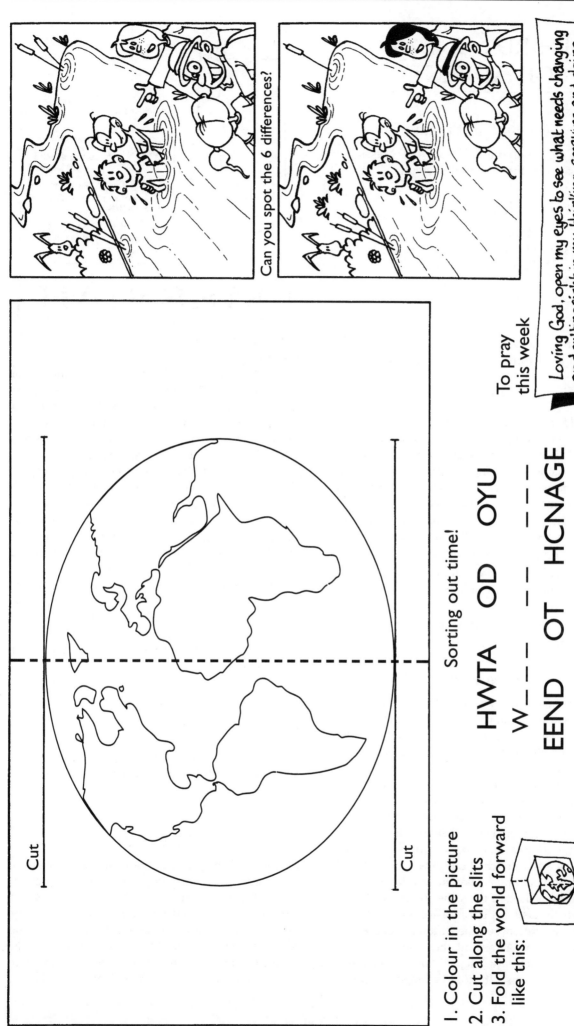

Can you spot the 6 differences!

To pray this week

Loving God, open my eyes to see what needs changing and putting right in my thinking, speaking and doing, because I want to turn away from sin, and turn towards you. Amen.

Cut

Cut

Sorting out time!

HWTA OD OYU
W_ _ _ _ _ _ _ _ _

EEND OT HCNAGE
_ _ _ _ _ _ _ _ _ _ _

NI OYRU FILE?
_ _ _ _ _ _ _ _ _ _ ?

1. Colour in the picture
2. Cut along the slits
3. Fold the world forward like this:

4. Stick onto last week's section like this:

THIRD SUNDAY OF ADVENT

Thought for the day

In Jesus, God will be fulfilling the Messianic prophecies about the promised Saviour.

Readings

Isaiah 61:1-4, 8-11
Psalm 126 or Canticle: Magnificat
1 Thessalonians 5:16-24
John 1:6-8, 19-28

Aim

To know that the prophets foretold the coming of Jesus, and Jesus fulfilled these prophecies.

Starter

The next object is . . . Have a number of objects hidden from view. Give out a short description of an item, such as: 'This object is black and white and re(a)d.' The children raise their hand when the item matching the description is shown. Show several other items before showing a newspaper, which fits the description, even though it may be slightly different from what was expected. Here are some other ideas:

- The next object has a face all the time (a clock)
- The next object is for the heads of li(e)rs (a pillow)
- The next object is to play with when you get round to it (a ball)
- The next object is put up at the down times (an umbrella)

Teaching

Talk about how we knew what to look out for in that game, so we could recognise the object when it appeared. And sometimes we understood the description better after we'd seen the object.

Today we are looking at some of the things the prophets said to describe the coming Messiah, long before Jesus was born. When Jesus did appear on earth, those things came true, and people found they understood them better than they had before.

On a large sheet of coloured paper, draw an outline of Jesus, his arms stretched out in welcome, based on the picture below, and lay this on the floor. On top of it have a sheet of the same size but different colour, which has been cut into sections. On each section have written out the different sections of Isaiah's prophecy. Across all these lay a title on white paper which says 'Messiah' on one side and 'Christ' on the reverse. It should all look like this:

Tell the good news to the poor	Comfort the broken-hearted
Set free those feeling imprisoned	Announce the time when God would show his merciful judgement
Give people clothes of praise and joy to replace their sadness	Be fair to everyone
Make what is right grow strong	Put wrong things right

MESSIAH

Explain how the prophets were sent by God to prepare the people for the coming of his chosen one. The Hebrew word for this anointed, chosen person was 'Messiah'. The Greek word was 'Christ'. (Turn the title over and back as you say this. Leave it on the Messiah side.) As the Old Testament is written in Hebrew, we'll stick with their word, Messiah, while they are waiting for him to come.

In order to help the people get ready, God spoke through the prophets to tell them what the Messiah would be like when he came. That way they could recognise him, and be ready for him. Let's look at some of the things they said about this Messiah. Lay the Messiah title at the side, and look at the sections, one by one, with all the readers reading them out. In turn take each section off and lay them all around the emerging picture. Gradually we can see that all these descriptions fit the Jesus we know from the Gospels. And as the New Testament was written in Greek, we'll use the Greek word for him: the Christ. (Reverse the title.)

Praying

Jesus, Jesus, we have come to see
that you must really be
the Son of God our Father.
We've been with you and we all agree
that only in your service
can the world be truly free!

Activities

On the sheet the preparations continue for the third stage of the Christmas pop-up model. Instructions and outlines are provided, but you may wish to strengthen the models with thin card. Also, if time permits, look at how the Bible is split into Old and New Testaments, and look at the names of the prophets, flicking through the Old Testament to find the books of Isaiah, Jeremiah and the others.

To pray this week

Jesus, Jesus,
we have come to see
that you must really be
the Son of God our Father.
We've been with you
and we all agree
that only in your service
can the world be truly free!

M C E H S R S I S A T H

Can you find the Hebrew and the Greek names for God's chosen one?

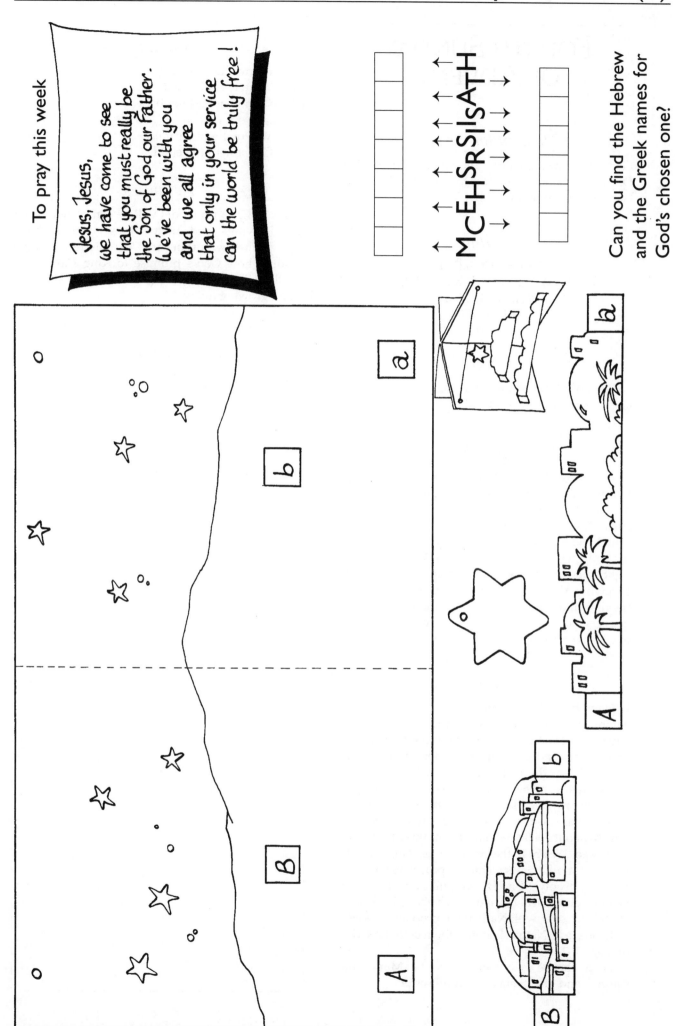

FOURTH SUNDAY OF ADVENT

Thought for the day

God's promised kingdom, announced both to King David in ancient times and to Mary by the angel Gabriel, will go on for ever.

Readings

2 Samuel 7, 1-11, 16
Canticle: Magnificat or Psalm 89:1-4, 19-26
Romans 16:25-27
Luke 1:26-38

Aim

To see how Gabriel's news to Mary fitted in with God's promise to King David.

Starter

Pass the ring. Thread a ring on a length of string. Everyone holds the string, passing it through their hands. One person stands in the middle of the circle. The ring gets passed secretly along the string from hand to hand. The person in the middle has to try and guess where it has got to. When they are right someone else takes over in the centre. Finish by giving a pack of sweets to whoever is holding the ring, and asking them to hand the sweets round to everyone, so that as the ring is revealed, everyone is given a gift.

Teaching

Explain that all through the hundreds of years before Jesus was born, God's promise had been passed on, from one generation to the next, sometimes seen and sometimes hidden from public view, until at the first Christmas, when Jesus the Christ was born, that message was seen clearly, and has been bringing blessing to everyone ever since.

But what was the message? Let's first go back in time to about 1000 BC – that's about three thousand years ago. We are in the city of Jerusalem, and this is King David. (Dress a child appropriately.) He is thinking deeply. (King David thinks deeply.) Then he has a good idea. (Turn on torch above his head.) He talks it over with Nathan the prophet. (Choose someone to be Nathan and give them both the script on page 131.)

Then choose two children to be Mary and Gabriel, and give them the second script.

Praying

Once in royal David's city
stood a lowly cattle shed,
where a mother laid her baby
in a manger for a bed.
Mary was that mother mild,
Jesus Christ her little child.

Activities

Today the pop-up model will be completed, using the drawings and instructions on the sheet, strengthened with thin card. Also discuss with the children how God's promise to King David was fulfilled when Mary said yes to God. Jesus' kingdom is still growing today.

Notes

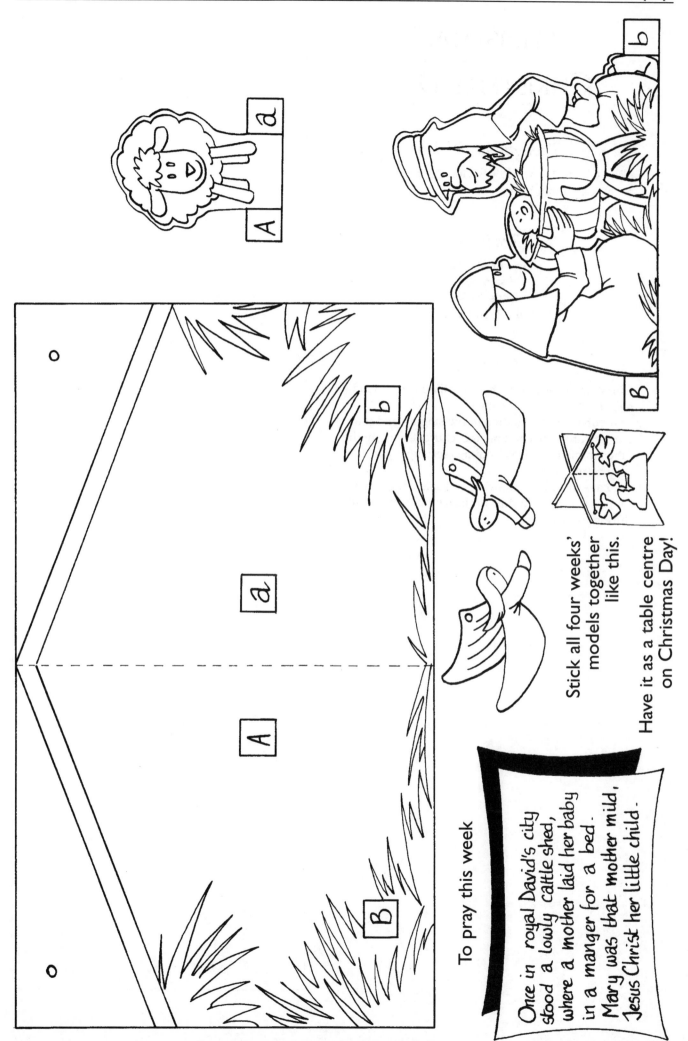

To pray this week

Once in royal David's city
stood a lowly cattle shed,
where a mother laid her baby
in a manger for a bed.
Mary was that mother mild,
Jesus Christ her little child.

Stick all four weeks'
models together
like this.

Have it as a table centre
on Christmas Day!

CHRISTMAS

CHRISTMAS DAY

Thought for the day

Jesus Christ, the world's Saviour, is here with us, born as a human baby.

Readings

Isaiah 62:6-12
Psalm 97
Titus 3:4-7
Luke 2:(1-7) 8-20

Activities

Christmas Day is very much a time for all God's children to worship together.

Involve all the children in the singing and playing of carols, decorating the church, and in the other ministries of welcoming, serving, collection of gifts and so on.

I have included a drawing and colouring activity for today so that children in church can work at this during the sermon.

Notes

To pray this week

Here in a manger,
newly-born and very small,
Jesus, our Saviour,
is laid.
Jesus, we welcome you
into our world.
Jesus, we welcome you
into our lives!

You will need:

a wide-necked jar

a tea light

a pair
of scissors

What you do
1. Colour and cut out the crib scene
2. Stick it round the *outside* of the jar
3. Light a candle inside the jar

One day ... God will come in person ... and live among us ... one day ...

NOW!

One day ... God will come in person ... and live among us ...

EMMANUEL – GOD WITH US

First Sunday of Christmas

Thought for the day

Just as the angels said, a Saviour has been born for us.

Readings

Isaiah 61:10-62:3
Psalm 148
Galatians 4:4-7
Luke 2:15-21

Aim

To celebrate that Jesus was born in the city of David, the shepherd boy king.

Starter

Play 'Simon says' but make it 'King David says'.

Teaching

Remind the children of when King David lived (about one thousand years before Jesus, which is about three thousand years ago). One way of doing this is placing four bricks spread out in a line across the whole floor as thousand year markers. Walk with the children from the first brick (which you can label 'King David' as you pass it) on to the second thousand years marker (labelled 'Jesus Christ') on to the third (labelled 'Battle of Hastings') until they reach the last marker (labelled 'Now!').

Dress one child as a shepherd boy. When David was a child, his job was to be out with the sheep in the fields near Bethlehem, looking after them (everyone makes bleating noises), keeping them safe from wolves and bears (wolves howling and bears growling), and leading them to the places where there was plenty of grass to eat, and water to drink (sheep eating and drinking noises).

A thousand years later, when Jesus was born, there were still shepherds in the fields near Bethlehem, looking after their sheep (bleating noises), keeping them safe from wolves and bears (wolves howling and bears growling), and leading them to the places where there was plenty of grass to eat and water to drink (sheep eating and drinking noises). As you know, Joseph was from King David's family, and that's why Joseph and Mary had come to David's home city of Bethlehem for the register. And, as you know, Jesus was born while they were there.

The angels could have told anyone about the birth of this baby, couldn't they? But who did they tell? It was the shepherds in the fields near Bethlehem, while they were at work, looking after their sheep, keeping them safe from wolves and bears, and leading them to the places where there was plenty of grass to eat and water to drink (appropriate noises).

When we read that the shepherds were the first to be told about the baby Jesus, it reminds us that:

1. Jesus grew up to be like a good shepherd, because he looks after us all, keeps us safe from evil, and leads us to where we can be spiritually fed and watered. (Place down a woolly lamb and a crook.)

2. Jesus is a 'son of David', born in David's city and of David's line, or family. (Place down a family tree with Luke's genealogy on it, showing David clearly at the top and Jesus at the bottom.)

3. Like David, Jesus is a King, not just for a while in history, but for ever. (Place down a crown.)

Praying

Jesus, born in David's city
born of David's line,
you are my shepherd
and you are my King.

Activities

On the sheet there are drawings and instructions to make shepherds, running to welcome Jesus. Colour the pictures first and stick them on to thin card so that they work properly. Each child will need a split pin for each running shepherd.

Notes

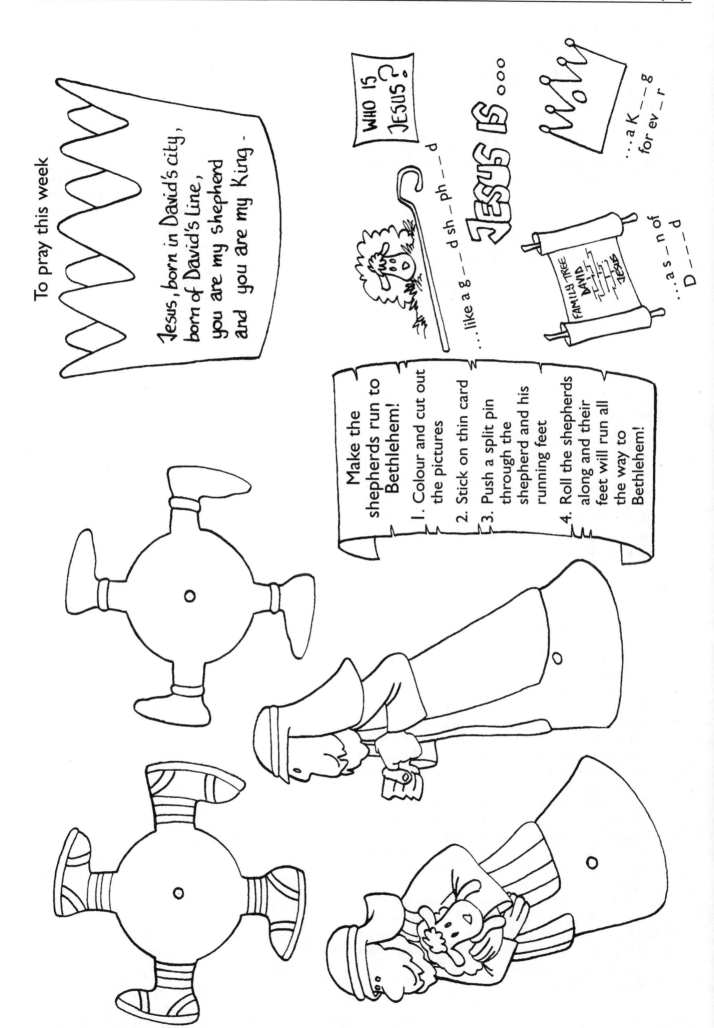

To pray this week

Jesus, born in David's city,
born of David's line,
you are my shepherd
and you are my King -

WHO IS JESUS?

JESUS IS ...

...like a g _ _ d sh _ ph _ _ d

... a K _ _ g for ev _ r

FAMILY TREE
DAVID

... a s _ _ n of D _ _ _ d

Make the shepherds run to Bethlehem!

1. Colour and cut out the pictures

2. Stick on thin card

3. Push a split pin through the shepherd and his running feet

4. Roll the shepherds along and their feet will run all the way to Bethlehem!

Second Sunday of Christmas

Thought for the day

The Word made flesh at Christmas was always with God, always expressing his creative love.

Readings

Jeremiah 31:7-14 or Ecclesiasticus 24:1-12
Psalm 147:12-20 or Canticle:
Wisdom of Solomon 10:15-21
Ephesians 1:3-14
John 1:(1-9) 10-18

Aim

To know that Jesus is sometimes called 'the Word of God'.

Starter

Play a simplified game of Pictionary, using a blackboard or sheets of lining paper fixed to the wall. Whisper the word to the first drawer and everyone shouts what they think it is. First to guess gets to draw next.

Teaching

As we saw, it's sometimes quite hard to know what someone is thinking if you can't use words. Words make it much easier for us to understand one another. That's what they're for. Ask them to give instructions for getting to somewhere close by – their school, for instance, or a well-known shop – and to give a description of a familiar object.

God wanted all the people he had made to understand that he really loved them. He wanted them to understand what God was really like. If we were to look at the world God made, what could we tell about him? (Collect their ideas.) So we can tell that God is generous and loving, careful and thorough, clever and organised, gentle and powerful, just by looking at the world, because it expresses what God is like, just as words do. It was through God's Word that all this came to exist.

Now show some Christmas cards with Jesus as a baby on them. Eventually, God's Word was not just spoken but actually lived. Jesus is sometimes known as the Word of God, because his life expressed exactly what God is like – a living Word for us to understand in our human language!

Praying

Word of the Father,
now in flesh appearing!
O come, let us adore him,
Christ the Lord.

Activities

There is an activity to look at the words we speak, and what message they give, and there are speech bubbles in which to draw God's Word, not just as a baby but also at other times of his life.

Notes

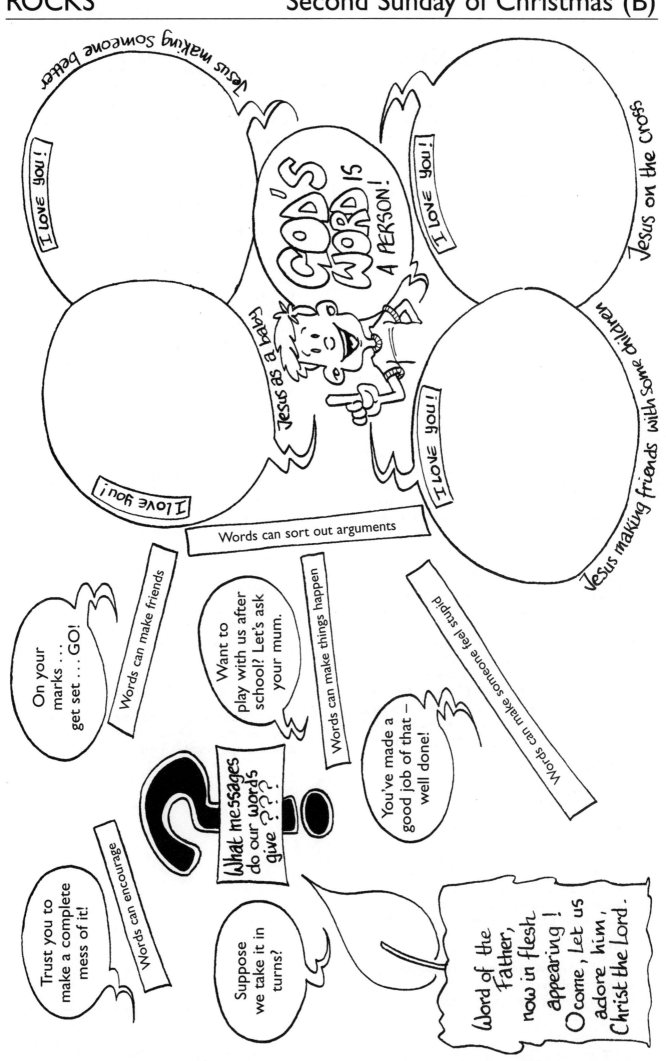

EPIPHANY

THE EPIPHANY

Thought for the day

Jesus, the promised Messiah, is shown to the Gentile world.

Readings

Isaiah 60:1-6
Psalm 72:(1-9) 10-15
Ephesians 3:1-12
Matthew 2:1-12

Aim

To understand that Jesus was being shown to the Gentiles as well as the Jewish people.

Starter

Sit in a circle, passing a locked box round to each in turn. As each one holds the box they say, 'One day I would love to go to . . . and see . . .' This can be a place or a person, a thing or an event, anywhere in the world or the universe. (Start it off yourself so they get the idea.)

Teaching

Share something or somewhere you had always hoped to see and which was different but even better than you had expected when you actually got to visit it. Today we are learning about some people who found what they were hoping to find, but it was all a bit different from what they expected.

Have everyone kneeling back on their heels, as in 'Do you want to go on a lion hunt', slapping their thighs with their hands to make the walking noise.

The children just repeat what you say.

Chorus
We're going on a journey . . .
a very long journey . . .
far away from home . . .
We're looking for a king.

We've noticed a star . . . *(point up)*
a very big star . . . *(look up, screwing up eyes)*
and we know it means a king!
Hold on! . . . We've come to a river . . .
Let's wade across . . . Swish, swish, swish.

Chorus

Hold on! . . . We've come to a mountain . . .
Let's climb over it . . .
  (do slow slaps up it and fast down the other side)

Chorus

We stopped at a palace . . . *(stop the 'walking')*
a very fine palace . . . *(bow to the ground)*
but there was no new king. *(shake head)*
Herod didn't know anything! *(shrug shoulders)*

Chorus

The star led us to Bethlehem . . . *(stop the walking)*
it led us to a house . . . *(point forward)*
a very ordinary house . . .
  (a 'can this be the right place' look!)
and we knocked at the door . . . *(clap three times)*

Chorus (changed to 'We've been on a journey')

And he's here!
We gave him our presents
  (carefully place gift on floor in front of you)
We bowed in worship *(bow to the ground)*
He wasn't in a palace . . .
  (resume the thigh slapping and shake head)
He isn't rich at all . . . *(shake head again)*
But he's king of the mountains and rivers . . .
  (speed up the thigh slapping)
and king of us all!
  (fast drumming on thighs, finishing with applause)

Praying

We bring you the GOLD
of our obedience.
Help us to live as you want us to.

We bring you the FRANKINCENSE
of our worship.
You are God and we worship you.

We bring you the MYRRH
of our world's sadness.
Help us look after one another better.
Amen.

Activities

On the sheet the children learn about the word 'Gentiles' and see the wise men's visit as Jesus being shown to the Gentile world.

Notes

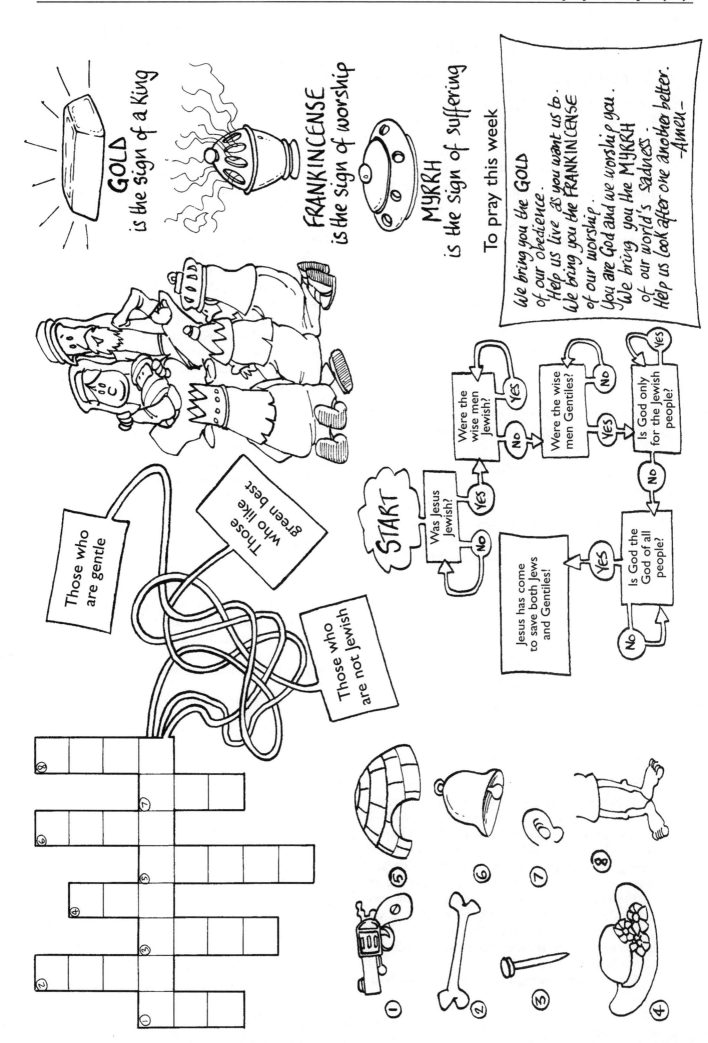

GOLD is the sign of a King

FRANKINCENSE is the sign of worship

MYRRH is the sign of suffering

To pray this week

We bring you the GOLD of our obedience. Help us live as you want us to. We bring you the FRANKINCENSE of our worship. You are God and we worship you. We bring you the MYRRH of our world's sadness. Help us look after one another better. —Amen—

Those who are gentle

Those who like green best

Those who are not Jewish

START

Was Jesus Jewish?

Were the wise men Jewish?

Were the wise men Gentiles?

Is God only for the Jewish people?

Is God the God of all people?

Jesus has come to save both Jews and Gentiles!

THE BAPTISM OF CHRIST: FIRST SUNDAY OF EPIPHANY

Thought for the day

Through the Holy Spirit, Jesus is affirmed at his Baptism as God's beloved Son, and we too are given the Spirit of God which affirms us as God's adopted daughters and sons.

Readings

Genesis 1:1-5
Psalm 29
Acts 19:1-7
Mark 1:4-11

Aim

To become familiar with Mark's account of Jesus' Baptism and the significance of the dove.

Starter

Give out long strips of crepe paper, or several sheets between a group, or use a parachute as the whole group. These things are waved in a way that expresses different moods, for example: angry, happy, gentle, excited, peaceful, wild, controlled, hopeful.

Teaching

Share this poem:

It's funny,
my puppy knows just how I feel.
When I'm happy he's yappy
and squirms like an eel.
When I'm grumpy he's slumpy
and stays at my heel.
It's funny,
my puppy knows just how I feel.

(Anon)

As humans we can feel all sorts of different things, and as God made us like him, and as Jesus showed us, we can tell that God also feels sad and happy, he's both peaceful and powerful, both gentle and strong. So the Spirit of God will show that too. Sometimes, like at the beginning of creation, we are told the Spirit of God was 'brooding over the face of the deep', full of love and hope for all that was going to be brought to life. (They can move their streamers like this, starting still, moving gently and then more powerfully.)

Today we are hearing about the time when Jesus was baptised. As they listen to the way Mark tells it, suggest they listen out for what mood the Spirit of God was in at this particular time. Use a clear translation to read today's Gospel; you may find it helps the children to have it projected on an OHP with a picture of water on an acetate behind it. Or have it written clearly on a blackboard with coloured chalks or on a length of wallpaper, with a 'watery' border drawn round it. Talk about the Spirit of God resting gently on Jesus, like a gentle white bird, and let them move the streamers to express this.

Everyone can read out together the words of God which Jesus heard as the Spirit rested on him.

Remind everyone of how the Spirit of God came at Pentecost, powerful and sounding like a great rushing wind and like fire. (Move the streamers or sheets like this.) The Spirit can come on all of us gently and powerfully, quietly or noisily. Sometimes the Spirit makes us feel suddenly very full of peace and calm, and other times it makes us feel full of excitement about Jesus and enthusiasm for following him no matter what.

Praying

Spirit of the living God,
I believe and trust in you,
and want to follow you all my life.
Come into my life and live there,
so that each day I may know you better
and love you more.
Amen.

Activities

On the sheet there are instructions for making a Holy Spirit mobile, with the Spirit of God expressed in the power of flame and the gentleness of a dove. Either copy the sheet on to thin card or mount it on thin card before tying on to cotton for hanging up.

Notes

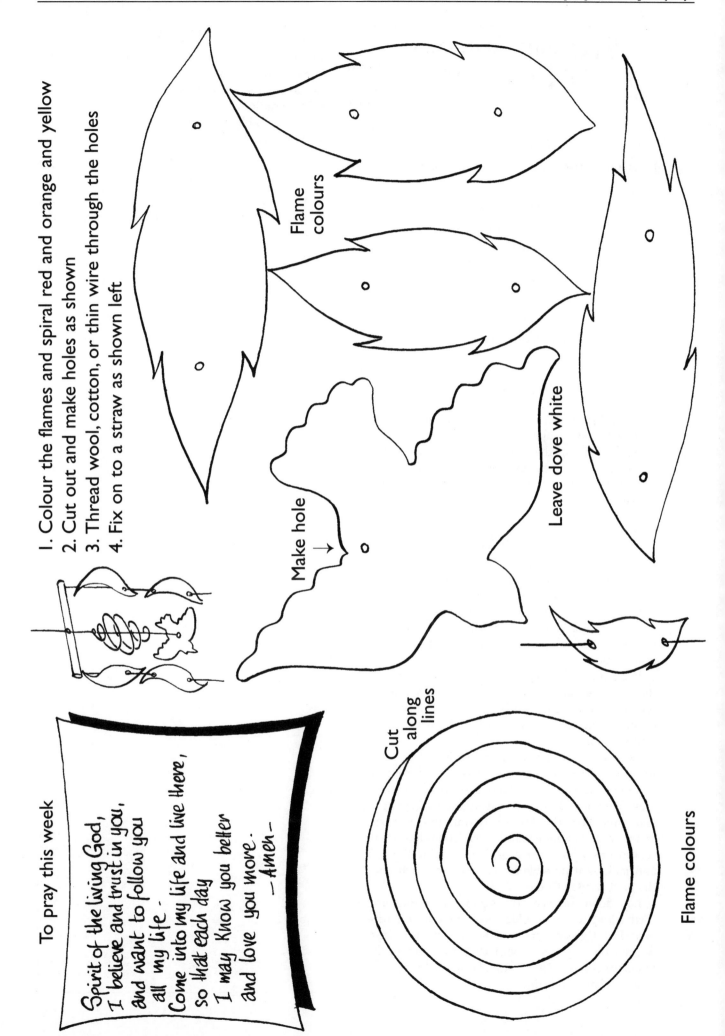

1. Colour the flames and spiral red and orange and yellow
2. Cut out and make holes as shown
3. Thread wool, cotton, or thin wire through the holes
4. Fix on to a straw as shown left

Flame colours

Make hole →

Leave dove white

Cut along lines

Flame colours

To pray this week

Spirit of the living God,
I believe and trust in you,
and want to follow you
all my life -
Come into my life and live there,
so that each day
I may know you better
and love you more.
— Amen —

SECOND SUNDAY OF EPIPHANY

Thought for the day

Jesus, the Christ, unlocks the mysteries of God.

Readings

1 Samuel 3:1-10 (11-20)
Psalm 139:1-6, 13-18
Revelation 5:1-10
John 1:43-51

Aim

To know that it is Jesus who bridges earth and heaven.

Starter

As a group build a bridge from newspaper. Get everyone rolling sheets of newspaper into firm sticks and fixing them together in a way that is strongest. (As far as possible, let the ideas come from the children, giving hints and nudges where necessary.)

Teaching

Why do we build bridges? When there's something which blocks you off from where you want to be, like a river or a railway, a bridge over it will let you get there and back easily. Bridges join places and people. They fill the gaps between people or places. To work properly, a bridge has to be touching both ends.

Place down two squares with a space between them. One square is covered with red dots and has the word 'Us' written in black on it. The other is covered with green dots and has the word 'God' written on it.

God is so holy and almighty that it is impossible for us to see God and live, so he is hidden from us. If we want to know what God is like, where can we look? We can look at the world around us, at people, and at the Bible. But if we really want to see clearly, in a way we can understand, what God is like, there is someone who is like a bridge, bridging the gap and making it possible for us to be in touch with the holy, hidden God.

Lay down between the squares and touching them a long rectangle which is covered in a mixture of red and green dots, and has the name 'Jesus' written on it. Jesus is both God and human, so when we choose to follow him he is able to show us clearly what God is like.

Praying

He came down to earth from heaven,
who is God and Lord of all,
and his shelter was a stable,
and his cradle was a stall;
with the humble, poor and lowly,
lived on earth our Saviour holy.

Activities

Using the sheet the children can make a model of a bridge which has the name of Jesus as part of the structure.

Notes

To pray this week

He came down to earth from heaven, who is God and Lord of all, and his shelter was a stable, and his cradle was a stall; with the humble, poor and lowly, lived on earth our Saviour holy.

Jesus bridges earth and heaven

1. Colour the bridge and the landscape

2. Fold the bridge like this

3. Stick A to A and B to B

Jesus is the bridge!

GOD

B

US

A

THIRD SUNDAY OF EPIPHANY

Thought for the day

Signs of glory lead us to believe in Jesus as Lord and Saviour.

Readings

Genesis 14:17-20
Psalm 128
Revelation 19:6-10
John 2:1-11

Aim

To know the story of the wedding at Cana.

Starter

Sit in a circle. The first person says, 'I went to a wedding and I saw . . .' and names one thing or person they saw. The next person repeats the sentence, adding another thing of their own, and so on around the circle.

Teaching

There are sound effects for the story today. Give a couple of children a bowl with water in it and two small pots. At appropriate times they can scoop up water and pour it out again. Give some other children instruments to play. Two children have wine glasses to clink as they say, 'Cheers!' At the asterisks, the children make the appropriate sounds.

Mary and Jesus and Jesus' friends were all invited to a wedding in Cana, which is a town in Galilee. When they got there the wedding music was playing cheerfully *. All the guests were chatting and laughing together *. There was plenty of delicious food to eat * and wine to drink *.

But then a terrible thing happened * (gasp). They ran out of wine * (gasp). Mary went and whispered to Jesus * and then she whispered to the servants *, telling them to do whatever Jesus told them to. Mary knew that Jesus would be able to help.

Jesus told the servants to fill the water pots with water, and the servants did as he said *. The wedding music continued to play cheerfully *. All the guests went on chatting and laughing *. None of them knew what the servants were doing. Then Jesus told the servants to go to the chief guest and pour out some of the water as wine, and they did as Jesus said *. He clinked glasses with his friends * and drank the water. But it wasn't water any more, it was top quality wine! * (gasp). It was the best wine he had ever tasted * (gasp). As the wedding music played on * and the guests chatted and laughed *, Mary and Jesus' friends and the servants smiled. This was the first of Jesus' miracles, and they had just seen it happen. (Everyone claps.)

Praying

Lord Jesus,
whenever we don't know what to do
or how to cope,
remind us to listen to you
and do whatever you tell us to.

Activities

On the sheet there is a wordsearch about the wedding at Cana, and a spot-the-difference picture of a Jewish wedding.

Notes

To pray this week

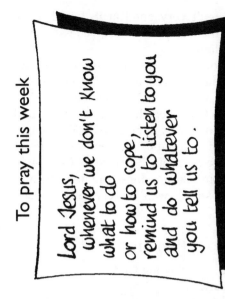

*Lord Jesus,
whenever we don't know
what to do
or how to cope,
remind us to listen to you
and do whatever
you tell us to.*

SPOT THE DIFFERENCE

There are 5 differences in these pictures of a Jewish wedding. Can you spot them?

Mary has some good advice for you. What is she saying? (John 2 verse 5)

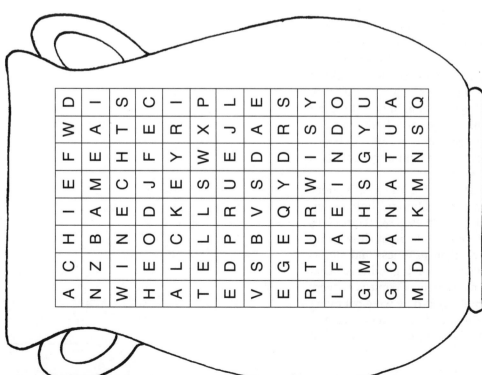

A	C	H	I	E	F	W	D
N	Z	B	A	M	E	A	I
W	I	N	E	C	H	T	S
H	E	O	D	J	F	E	C
A	L	C	K	E	Y	R	I
T	E	L	L	S	W	X	P
E	D	P	R	U	E	J	L
V	S	B	V	S	D	A	E
E	G	E	Q	Y	D	R	S
R	T	U	R	W	I	S	Y
L	F	A	E	I	N	D	O
G	M	U	H	S	G	Y	U
G	C	A	N	A	T	U	A
M	D	I	K	M	N	S	Q

JESUS   MARY   CHIEF   CANA
GUEST   WEDDING   DISCIPLES
WATER   WINE   JARS
DO   WHATEVER   HE   TELLS   YOU

FOURTH SUNDAY OF EPIPHANY

Thought for the day

Jesus displays all the signs that mark him out to be God's chosen One.

Readings

Deuteronomy 18:15-20
Psalm 111
Revelation 12:1-5a
Mark 1:21-28

Aim

To recognise that the shining light of God's goodness shows up evil and challenges it.

Starter

Make the room as dark as possible, and have a powerful torch. The children start at one end of the room and try to creep up to you without you seeing them moving in the light of the torch, which you sweep like a searchlight slowly back and forth across the room. Anyone caught moving in the light has to come and help you check for other movers.

Teaching

Flash the torch around again and talk together about how light shows up things which are hidden in the darkness. When might we be pleased to have the light spotting us? (If we were shipwrecked and wanting to be rescued; if we were lost in a dark wood; if we're doing something we're proud of; if we're dressed in our coolest clothes.) When might we not want the light to spot us and show us up? (If we're doing something we know we shouldn't be doing; if we're wearing something awful; if we're up to no good.) The thing about light is that it can't help showing everything up clearly, both the good and the bad. Shine a torch into a dark cupboard and it might show up either a ten pound note or a dead mouse the cat has brought in!

When Jesus went about on earth, God's glory couldn't help shining out of him and lighting up people's souls to them, so they saw themselves clearly, as they really were. God's light showed up to them very clearly all their nastiness and sin, as well as all their loveliness and goodness. That wasn't always a very nice feeling. People who were behaving badly, but pretended they were behaving well, found Jesus' light showing up their lies and they hated it. People who longed to live well, but knew they weren't very good at it, found Jesus' light showing them hope and forgiveness, and so they loved the light.

God's light still shines. It still shows up to us our nastiness and sin, as well as our loveliness and goodness. How are we going to feel about that?

If we were to hate everything good, honest and right, then we would do our best to shut God's light out, so the evil in us could be safely hidden to fester and grow in darkness again. But if we see God's light as a way of helping the goodness and honesty in us to grow tall and strong, we'll be very happy to let it shine in us.

Praying

All-seeing God, all-knowing God,
shine in my heart,
so that the goodness grows strong
and no evil can take root.

Activities

On the sheet the children are helped to explore the story of today's Gospel, and in a colouring activity they can spot the signs which lead them to uncover a great truth.

Notes

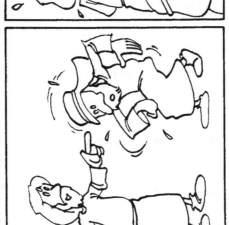

'What's going on? This Jesus speaks with God's authority and even the evil spirits do what he says!' The people talked about Jesus everywhere.

On the Sabbath day Jesus went to the synagogue and began to teach. Everyone was amazed at his teaching.

A man who had an evil spirit in him shouted at Jesus, 'Jesus of Nazareth! What do you want with us? Did you come to destroy us? I know who you are!'

Jesus said strongly, 'Be quiet! Come out of the man!' The evil spirit shook the man, gave a loud cry and left him.

Use Mark 1:21-28 to match the captions with the pictures

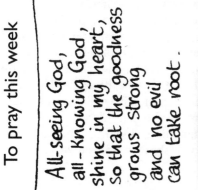

To pray this week

All-seeing God,
all-knowing God,
shine in my heart,
so that the goodness
grows strong
and no evil
can take root.

WHO IS THIS JESUS PERSON?

To find out, colour the R's red
the B's blue
the Y's yellow
the O's orange
the G's green

ORDINARY TIME

PROPER 1

Sunday between 3 and 9 February inclusive
(if earlier than the Second Sunday before Lent)

Thought for the day

The good news about God is far too good to keep to ourselves.

Readings

Isaiah 40:12-31
Psalm 147:1-11, 20c
1 Corinthians 9:16-23
Mark 1:29-39

Aim

To see how keen Jesus is to spread the good news of God's kingdom.

Starter

In another room or behind a screen have an assembled picture based on the one below, composed of various sections of coloured paper arranged in layers. Beside the picture have all the component parts of a replica picture, already cut. (Have enough for several pictures if you have a large group, and sort the children into teams.)

In the main room, explain that their task is to put together here the same picture as is hidden, and it must be made up in the right order. One child at a time can go and look at the finished picture and choose *one* piece to bring back, which they reckon is the next to be placed. Then another child can collect the next piece and so on. If they find the wrong piece

has been collected, that must be returned before another piece is chosen. Eventually the two pictures can be shown together to check they are the same.

Teaching

Have two of the leaders pretending to be Peter and his mother-in-law. Mother-in-law is stirring a pot in which she's cooking supper, and Peter is sewing a sail. They talk about when supper will be ready, and start remembering the time when mother-in-law was so ill that she couldn't get up, and she had invited Jesus to supper. Together they chat their way through, remembering that amazing evening, with Jesus arriving, how he was so kind to her, and then how she felt when Jesus healed her. She can probably remember exactly what meal she cooked for them all! Then they remember all the other people coming, crowding round the door. (How did they know? Had mother-in-law met someone and told them what had happened to her?)

They go on to remember how Jesus was missing the next morning and Peter had gone looking for him and found him praying in the hills. What was it he said? Why was it he wanted to leave their town and go travelling around?

Make the conversation natural, asking each other questions and adding any character details that seem appropriate. Then freeze for a few seconds, leave the acting place and join the group as ordinary leaders again. Let the children relate to you what Jesus had been up to, and why he wanted to travel around. (So that lots of other people would be able to find out what it was like to know God's healing in their lives.)

In the picture we made earlier, we could only come back with the right information when we had seen the finished picture, and knew what we were doing. Jesus knew God so completely that he could show people exactly what God was like, even to the point of loving them to full health again. The closer we get to God, the more clearly we'll be able to show other people what God is like – by the way *we* are speaking and listening, looking, thinking and behaving. What will show is God's love.

Praying

Jesus, send us out to make God's love known,
so that more and more people
can meet you and enjoy living as your friend.

Activities

On the sheet there is a chart to help the children think through the methods of communication open to us, and which are most appropriate for giving information to small and large numbers of people. This leads them to think about how their lives can communicate God's love to others, rather than simply talking about God.

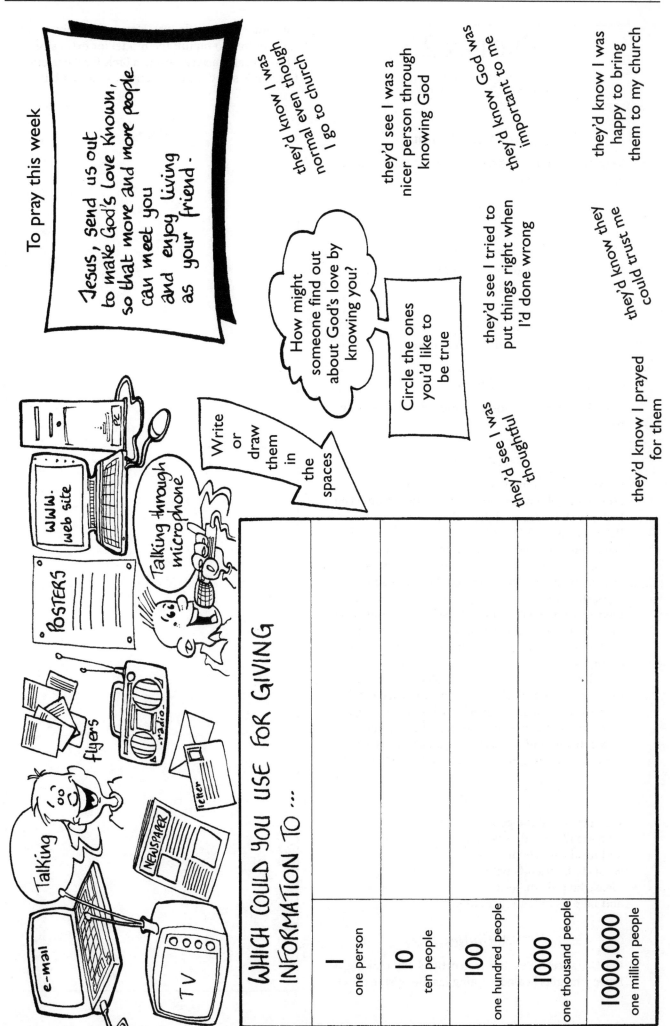

To pray this week

Jesus, send us out to make God's love known, so that more and more people can meet you and enjoy living as your friend.

How might someone find out about God's love by knowing you?

Circle the ones you'd like to be true

they'd know I was normal even though I go to church

they'd see I was a nicer person through knowing God

they'd know God was important to me

they'd know I was happy to bring them to my church

they'd see I tried to put things right when I'd done wrong

they'd know they could trust me

they'd see I was thoughtful

they'd know I prayed for them

Write or draw them in the spaces

WHICH COULD YOU USE FOR GIVING INFORMATION TO...

1 one person	
10 ten people	
100 one hundred people	
1000 one thousand people	
1,000,000 one million people	

e-mail

TV

Talking

Newspaper

letter

flyers

radio

POSTERS

www. web site

Talking through microphone

PROPER 2

*Sunday between 10 and 16 February inclusive
(if earlier than the Second Sunday before Lent)*

Thought for the day

Jesus wants to heal us to wholeness, and to him no one is untouchable.

Readings

2 Kings 5:1-14
Psalm 30
1 Corinthians 9:24-27
Mark 1:40-45

Aim

To know the story of the healed leper.

Starter

Play 'Piggy in the middle' using soft balls or bean-bags.

Teaching

Begin by explaining to the children what leprosy is. (You can get posters and information from The Leprosy Mission, Goldhay Way, Orton Goldhay, Peterborough PE2 5GZ.) They also need to understand what the law said about those suffering from leprosy. They were considered 'unclean' and so was anyone who touched them, so all lepers had to live separately and warn people to keep away from them by calling out, 'Unclean! Unclean!' The law also said that if a leper got better, he had to show himself to the priest, who would officially pronounce him clean again.

Tell the story, or have it narrated, as you draw the events on a blackboard. You don't have to be brilliant at drawing – it just helps to focus their listening, and aids remembering. The advantage of a blackboard and chalk is that you can erase easily, not only mistakes, but also spots on cured lepers!

Praying

We pray for all the people
who are ill, or sad, or lonely,
and for those who no one
wants to be friends with.
Please help them, Jesus,
and help us to help them too.

Activities

On the sheet there are instructions for making a leper who gets healed, turning his life upside down (or rather down side up). Have some thin card for the children to mount the model for extra strength. They will also need access to a Bible for the references to today's story, and the activity to go with it.

Notes

To pray this week

We pray for all the people who are ill, or sad, or lonely, and for those who no one wants to be friends with –
Please help them, Jesus, and help us to help them too.

Look at Mark 1 verse 41

Look at Mark 1 verse 40

Jesus heals a leper!

How to make a model of Naaman getting healed

1. Colour Naaman and cut him out. If you like, stick him on to thin card.

2. Colour his tunic and stick flap A on to the middle of Naaman.

3. Now you can see Naaman's spots clear up, just by turning him upside down.

Turn Naaman's life upside down to see what happened to him!

A

Stick A here

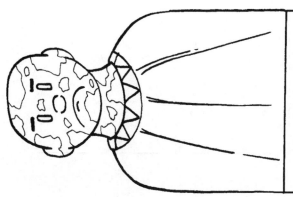
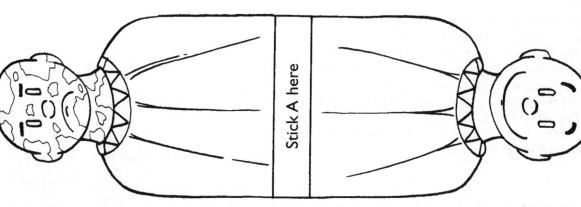

Proper 3

Sunday between 17 and 23 February inclusive
(if earlier than the Second Sunday before Lent)

Thought for the day

The Son of Man has authority on earth to forgive sins.

Readings

Isaiah 43:18-25
Psalm 41
2 Corinthians 1:18-22
Mark 2:1-12

Aim

To look at Jesus' authority to forgive sins.

Starter

Simon says. Point out that Simon is the only one with authority to tell us what to do.

Teaching

Act out the story of the paralysed man, with most children being the crowd, and a couple being scribes. The four friends climbing the outside stairs and making a hole in the roof is done with sound effects, and everyone looks up and follows the (imaginary) man's journey down to the floor. Give the scribes their thought bubble card so they can read it out, and give Jesus his speech bubble card. Then gather in a circle.

Place the thought and speech bubbles in the centre of the group, and read the scribes' thoughts out again. Explain that forgiveness means drowning someone's sins in perfect goodness and love, so only someone who is perfect in goodness and love can do it.

Were the scribes right in thinking that only God can forgive sins? Yes, they were. (You could read the children verse 25 from Isaiah 43, where God is speaking, through his prophet.)

Now look at what Jesus said. Why was Jesus able to forgive the man's sins? Because he really was God's Son.

Praying

Jesus Christ,
we have come to see
that you must really be
the Son of God our Father.
You love as the Father loves
and you forgive as the Father forgives.

Activities

On the sheet there is a wordsearch which reinforces their thinking about Jesus' authority, and a wild and desolate desert for them to bring to life, following the Isaiah reading. They will need access to a Bible for this.

Notes

ONLY GOD CAN FORGIVE SINS AND HERE IS JESUS DOING IT. WHO CAN HE BE?

How was this man a bit like the desert? How did Jesus change it for him?

Isaiah 43:18-21, and 25

Make this desert look as God promises it will in Isaiah 43

Suppose the desert is a picture of how people sometimes feel ...what does God promise to do?

DEEP THOUGHTS!

A	O	X	R	D	G	O	D	E	U
U	M	S	T	O	V	S	N	K	N
F	J	N	C	I	D	O	T	L	V
O	B	I	D	N	B	I	T	M	Y
R	E	S	P	G	Q	F	W	H	O
G	R	W	H	E	R	E	A	Z	L
I	C	I	G	C	A	N	K	I	Q
V	H	D	H	J	E	S	U	S	S
E	N	L	E	N	J	Y	F	P	G
A	S	I	H	C	A	N	B	E	?

To pray this week

Jesus Christ, we have come to see that you must really be the Son of God our Father. You love as the Father loves, and you forgive as the Father forgives.

SECOND SUNDAY BEFORE LENT

Thought for the day

Christ is the image of the unseen God.

Readings

Proverbs 8:1, 22-31
Psalm 104:24-35
Colossians 1:15-20
John 1:1-14

Aim

To marvel at God's creation, spoken into being through Love.

Starter

Have a selection of earth's wonders to enjoy, such as bubbles that are so light that they float about in the air, things that sink and float, prisms that split the light into rainbows, and 'fly eye' lenses that split the world into repeated images, wine glasses of water through which images turn upside down, and spoons which give distorted and upturned reflections.

Teaching

Gather around the objects once everyone has had time to experiment, and talk together about how the physical laws of our universe, which God has made, make these things happen, allow aeroplanes to fly, and let us stick safely on our planet without floating off into space. If you have a member of the congregation who is specially enthused by science, you could ask them along to join you, as you spend some time marvelling at it all. Whoever thought and loved all this into being, and keeps it going, must be amazingly wise, and different from anything we can imagine. He must be more than super-human, more than super-clever, more than super-imaginative. He must be outside time as we know it, as well as inside, and he must know all of us far better than we can ever know him. The name we give to this amazing great being is the Lord God Almighty, and he is so wonderful that we worship him.

Praying

Glory be to the Father
and to the Son
and to the Holy Spirit,
as God was in the beginning,
is NOW
and shall be for ever!

Activities

On the sheet there are instructions for another scientific investigation: growing a crystal tree. The children will need alum crystals dissolved in a little water, blotting paper cut into a tree shape as shown on the sheet, and shallow pots to stand the trees in. There is also a set of questions to get them thinking about ordinary things in a new way, and the prayer can be made beautiful with colouring or collage.

Notes

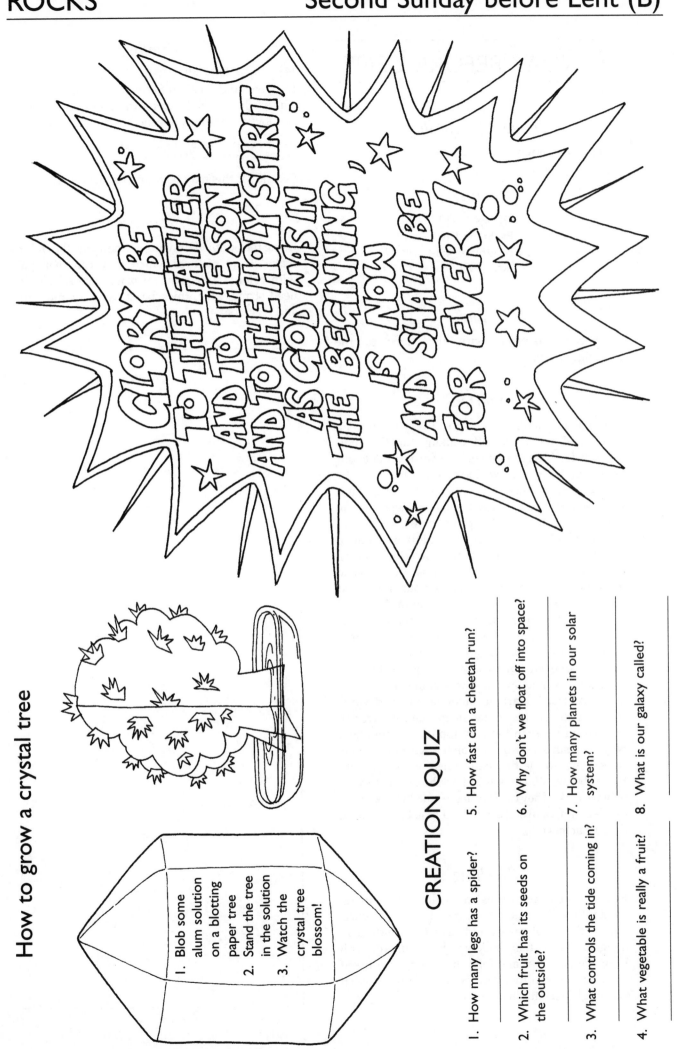

GLORY BE TO THE FATHER AND TO THE SON AND TO THE HOLY SPIRIT, AS GOD WAS IN THE BEGINNING, IS NOW AND SHALL BE FOR EVER!

How to grow a crystal tree

1. Blob some alum solution on a blotting paper tree
2. Stand the tree in the solution
3. Watch the crystal tree blossom!

CREATION QUIZ

1. How many legs has a spider?

2. Which fruit has its seeds on the outside?

3. What controls the tide coming in?

4. What vegetable is really a fruit?

5. How fast can a cheetah run?

6. Why don't we float off into space?

7. How many planets in our solar system?

8. What is our galaxy called?

SUNDAY BEFORE LENT

Thought for the day

God's glory shows.

Readings

2 Kings 2:1-12
Psalm 50:1-6
2 Corinthians 4:3-6
Mark 9:2-9

Aim

To become familiar with the story of the Transfiguration.

Starter

Climb a mountain on the spot. Everyone finds a space, and we all set off walking (on the spot) towards the high mountain. We stop and shade our eyes from the sun as we look up at the top in the distance; *that's* where we're going! As we go on it gets steeper . . . and steeper . . . and steeper . . . till we're struggling to walk upright. Soon we have to use our hands as well as our feet. Now we come to a high cliff face. We look up at it towering over us, and feel the cold rock with our hands. We'll have to be very careful, and find a hold for our right hand . . . then our left . . . then pull up on our feet and quickly find a new handhold . . . and another . . . as we make our way up the cliff face. When we climb over on to the top we've got to walk along a really narrow ledge. We flatten our hands against the rock to steady us, and move slowly along the narrow ledge. At last it starts to broaden out, and we're nearly at the top. It's not too steep, here, and we run the last bit to reach the very top of the mountain. Now we can stand on top of the world and look right down to the tiny path where we started off, far, far below. We can see far into the distance every way we look. (They can stay at the top, do the journey down again, or abseil down, and look back at what they've achieved.)

Teaching

Everyone lies face in arms on the floor, as we imagine a rather different kind of mountain experience. Play some quiet music and lead the children in imagination on that walk up the mountain with Jesus, Peter, James and John, imagining it yourself as you speak, so that it rings true. Think of what you might see and hear and feel.

Praying

Holy, most holy, all holy the Lord,
in power and wisdom for ever adored!
The earth and the heavens are full of your love;
our joyful hosannas re-echo above!

(From the 'Slane Sanctus' by Michael Forster
© 1995 Kevin Mayhew Ltd.)

(Music for this may be found on page 132.)

Activities

Using the outlined drawing on the sheet, the children make string pictures which they can then paint with colours and print on black paper. They will need string, glue, thick paint, card for mounting, and black paper.

Notes

Can you put God's words together so they make an important message!

This beloved to my him listen is Son.

What you do

1. Stick string along the lines

2. Paint over with bright coloured thick paint

3. Press black paper carefully over the picture to print out a sign of God's glory!

Print out God's glory

You will need:

string

bright coloured paint

PAINT

glue stick

GLUE

black paper

To pray this week

Holy, most holy, all holy the Lord,
in power and wisdom for ever
adored!
The earth and the heavens are
full of your love;
our joyful hosannas re-echo
above!

(From the 'Slane Sanctus' by Michael Forster
© 1995 Kevin Mayhew Ltd.)

LENT

FIRST SUNDAY OF LENT

Thought for the day

After his Baptism Jesus is led by the Spirit into the wilderness before returning to proclaim God's kingdom.

Readings

Genesis 9:8-17
Psalm 25:1-10
1 Peter 3:18-22
Mark 1:9-15

Aim

To think about the value of Jesus going into the desert after his Baptism.

Starter

Getting your bearings. Draw a large compass, showing the different directions clearly, and fix it to the middle of the floor. Everyone stands in a space and the leader calls out instructions – go two paces north, one pace south-east, two paces west, and so on.

Teaching

Mix up the separate letters of these words on the floor and get the children to help sort them into order: Who? What? How? Explain that Lent is a time for thinking about some big questions, and here are three big questions to start us off. Talk together with the children about plans for their lives. What kind of person do they want to be? (Who) What do they think they would like to do with their lives? (What) How are they hoping to do it? (How)

Then spread a large desert-coloured sheet or towel on the floor in the centre of the circle, keeping the words visible, and explain that as soon as Jesus had been baptised and filled with the Spirit of God, he felt led to go off on his own into the desert. (Place a small picture of Jesus somewhere on the desert, so that the emptiness and aloneness is emphasised to them.) And he lived there for forty days – about six weeks. While he was there he didn't eat. He wanted to clear his life completely for a while so he could give his whole attention to God.

Why did he want to do that? Because he wanted to listen to God very carefully, and find out *who* he was, *what* God wanted him to do in his life on earth, and *how* he should set about doing it. He knew they were hard questions, and wouldn't be easy to tackle,

but he knew it had to be done so his life wouldn't be wasted or go off in the wrong direction.

As you look at Jesus, remembering him taking time to find out how his life could best be lived, pray for each other's lives, that God will make it clear to us how they can best be lived, and what he would like us to do in them.

At the end of Jesus' forty days in the desert, he had travelled a very long way, not just on foot over the sand and scrub land, but also in his mind and his heart. And now he was ready to go back into the towns and villages to start his work – God's work – of loving and caring for people, teaching them and helping them get to know God and themselves better.

Praying

Heavenly Father,
my life stretches ahead of me,
full of hopes and ideas and dreams.
Please help me to understand myself,
show me how you would like me to live,
and what you would like me to do. Amen.

Activities

On the sheet there is a map of a desert for the children to work out the safe way to cross it, based on compass directions, and there are instructions for making a special compass that will keep them in God's direction through their lives.

Notes

---

a lid

split pin

colour and cut out

How to make a LIFE COMPASS to guide you through every desert!

LOVE GOD

LOVE GOD

To pray this week

Heavenly Father,
my life stretches ahead of me,
full of hopes and ideas and dreams.
Please help me to understand myself,
show me how you would like me
to live,
and what you would like me
to do.   —Amen—

Which way through the desert?

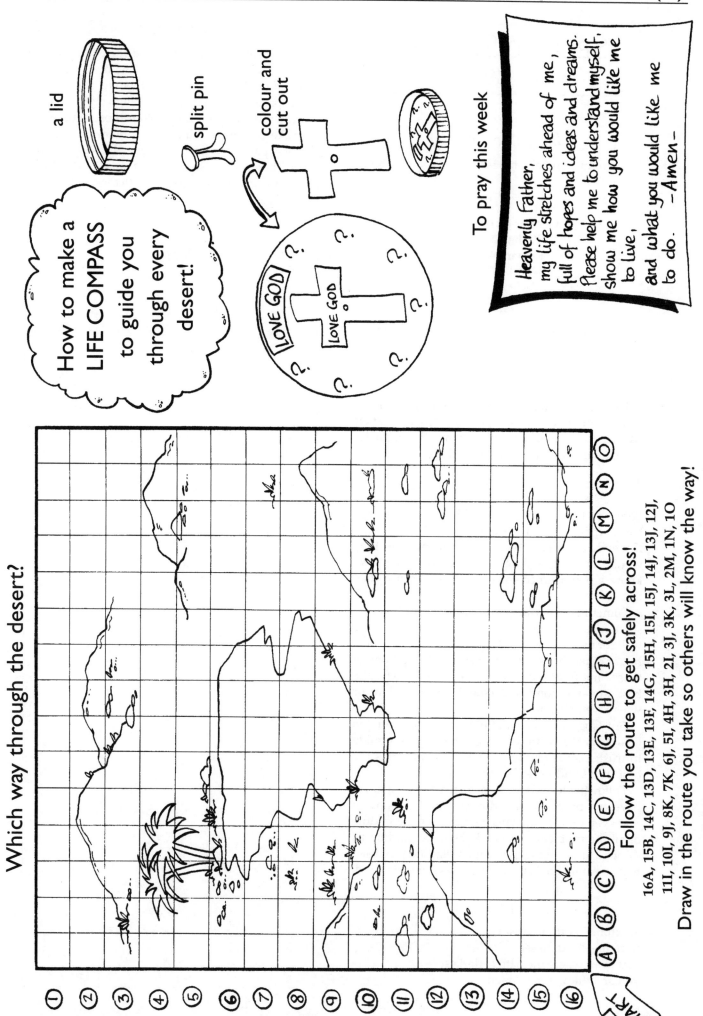

Ⓐ Ⓑ Ⓒ Ⓓ Ⓔ Ⓕ Ⓖ Ⓗ Ⓘ Ⓙ Ⓚ Ⓛ Ⓜ Ⓝ Ⓞ

① ② ③ ④ ⑤ ⑥ ⑦ ⑧ ⑨ ⑩ ⑪ ⑫ ⑬ ⑭ ⑮ ⑯

START

Follow the route to get safely across!
16A, 15B, 14C, 13D, 13E, 13F, 14G, 15H, 15I, 15J, 14J, 13J, 12J,
11I, 10I, 9J, 8K, 7K, 6J, 5I, 4H, 3H, 2I, 3J, 3K, 3L, 2M, 1N, 1O
Draw in the route you take so others will know the way!

SECOND SUNDAY OF LENT

Thought for the day

A commitment of faith has far-reaching implications.

Readings

Genesis 17:1-7, 15-16
Psalm 22:23-31
Romans 4:13-25
Mark 8:31-38

Aim

To know that we can always trust God, even in the difficult times.

Starter

Put some obstacles around. The children work in pairs, with one of each pair blindfolded. Their partner leads them carefully around the obstacles so that they don't bump into anything.

Teaching

Point out that because we couldn't see clearly, we had to trust our partners to lead us safely through. If they had not been interested in helping us, they would have let us down. We trust those who we know are concerned for our safety because they like us.

Sometimes life can be fun and easy and we can see where we're going, and everything's working well for us at home, at school and with our friends. But at other times, it can feel as if we've got one of those blindfolds on; we can't see what to do for the best, and we don't understand where we are or where we're heading.

But God is never blindfolded or asleep, or too busy to bother with us, so he's the very best guide to trust; because he loves us he always wants the best for us and never lets us down.

Following Jesus doesn't mean that we shall never have any problems or bad days. But it does mean that even on the bad days, and even in the middle of all the problems, Jesus will be there guiding us through and helping us to cope well. God promised that he would do this, and he always keeps his word.

Praying

Teach me, Lord, to trust you,
train me, Lord, to see
that even where the path is darkest
you are guiding me. Amen.

Activities

On the sheet there is a grid, and the children can't see the solution to the puzzle. The only way they can find out is by you guiding them to colour in the right spaces on the grid. So, in bingo style, you call out the numbers and they colour those squares in, to make the shape which helps them understand the first part of today's Gospel – the shape of the cross. There are also some 'desert questions' to think about and a cartoon version of the second part of the Gospel.

Notes

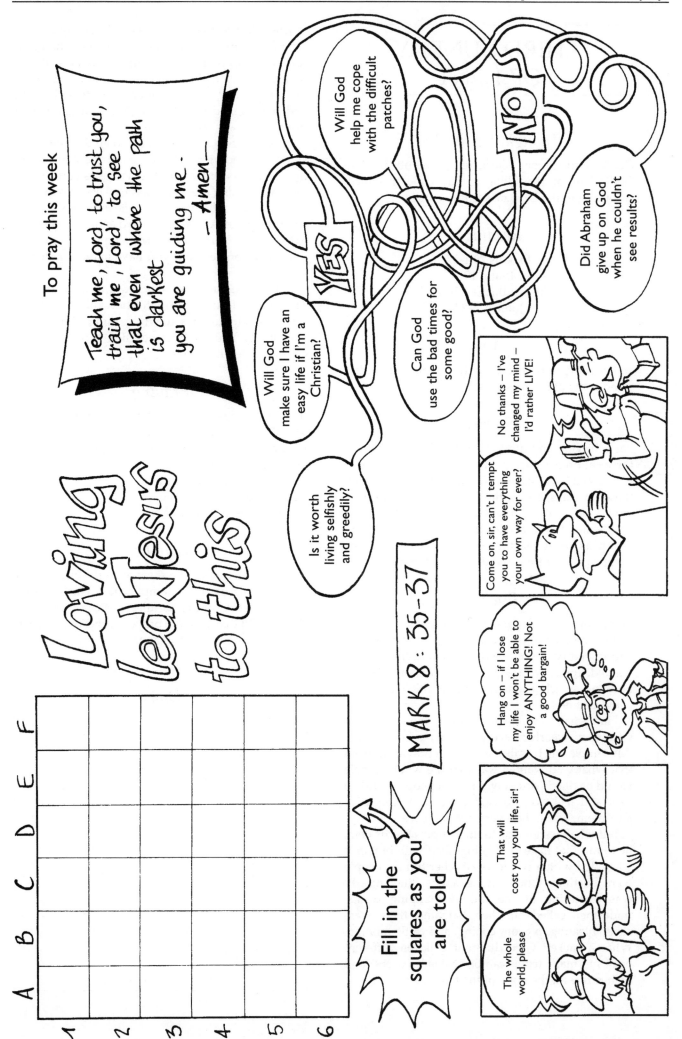

Third Sunday of Lent

Thought for the day

God's wisdom may shock us. Jesus, obedient to God's Law and fulfilling it, dies a death which, according to the Law, makes him cursed.

Readings

Exodus 20:1-17
Psalm 19
1 Corinthians 1:18-25
John 2:13-22

Aim

To know the story of Jesus in the temple, and understand some of the reasons for it.

Starter

An emptying and filling activity. Give each two or three children a small pot full of dried peas, a jug of water and two straws. To prevent spillage, put these on trays, fixing the pot of peas to the tray with a piece of blutack. The aim is to fill the pot with water, but to do this they first have to empty it of peas, using the straw-sucking method to pick up one pea at a time and drop it on the tray.

Teaching

Point out that we couldn't fill the pots with water at first because they were full up with peas; we had to empty the pot before we could fill it as we wanted. Today we are going to hear about a whole building which needed to be emptied before it could be filled!

Find Isaiah 56 verse 7 in the Bible, and also have it written out clearly so everyone can read it together: 'My temple will be called a house of prayer.' Explain that what God wanted was that the whole temple would be filled with prayer, so that people could go to it and feel close to God there. The temple, at Jerusalem, was to be a very special place.

But when Jesus came to the temple at Jerusalem, he found that instead of being filled with prayer it was filled with a whole lot of other things. People were bustling about buying and selling; money was clattering at the money-changing desks, tradesmen called out their bargains; there were sheep bleating, pigeons cooing, and cattle mooing. What a racket! Give different children different noises to make (coins can be shaken in a pot) and orchestrate all the noise of the temple.

Jesus knew that this was the last thing the temple was meant to be like, because God had said (everyone joins in), 'My temple will be called a house of prayer.' There was only one thing to do; the temple had to be emptied of all this cheating and buying and selling so it could be filled with prayer as it was meant to be.

As God's Son, Jesus strode into all the noise and started upending the tables so all the coins went flying (do this with a couple of tables as you speak), and overturning the boxes and baskets, driving out all the people who were using the temple of God as a market place. And as he walked about, he shouted to the people, 'It is written, "My temple will be called a house of prayer", but you have made it a den of thieves!'

All the people were shocked and a bit scared. They knew Jesus was right. They knew they had filled the temple up with wrong things. But now it was empty, and ready to be filled with prayer, as God intended it to be.

Praying

Jesus, my life is filled with lots of thoughts,
lots of words and lots of activities.
Please show me which of them are good
and which are not,
so I can be like God's temple,
empty of anything wrong
and filled with your love.

Activities

There is a picture on the sheet of all the buying and selling going on in the temple court. On the other side the same outline is filled with nothing, and they can fill that with the prayer suggested. The ten commandments are also taught.

Notes

To pray this week

Jesus, my life is filled with lots of thoughts, lots of words and lots of activities.
Please show me which of them are good and which are not, so I can be like God's temple, empty of anything wrong and filled with your love.

GOD'S RULES

LOVE GOD

1.
2.
3.
4.

AND

LOVE ONE ANOTHER

5.
6.
7.
8.
9.
10.

ISAIAH 56:7

JOHN 2:16

My temple shall be called a house of prayer . . . | . . . how dare you turn it into a market!

Colour in both pictures and stick the backs together

6. Do not kill

5. Honour your father and mother

9. Don't lie about people

7. Be faithful in all relationships

3. Don't use God's name badly

1. Love God with heart, soul, mind and strength

2. Don't worship idols

8. Do not steal

4. Keep God's day holy and special

10. Don't keep wanting what others have

FOURTH SUNDAY OF LENT: MOTHERING SUNDAY

Thought for the day

God provides comfort in all our troubles and sufferings.

Readings

Exodus 2:1-10 or 1 Samuel 1:20-28
Psalm 34:11-20 or Psalm 127:1-4
2 Corinthians 1:3-7 or Colossians 3:12-17
Luke 2:33-35 or John 19:25-27

Activities

Today is not one for learning separately but for celebrating and learning together. Use some of the all-age suggestions from the *Living Stones* Complete Resource Book, involve the children and young people in the music group or choir, as servers, welcomers, collectors for the offering, and so on. Provide shakers and bells for the younger ones to play during one or two hymns, and streamers to wave. Gather the children round the altar for the eucharistic prayer and choose hymns where the language is accessible.

Notes

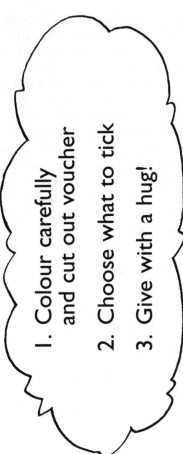

1. Colour carefully and cut out voucher

2. Choose what to tick

3. Give with a hug!

Dear Mum,
I remember when you comforted me ... thanks
for loving me !

Draw it here ↻

MOTHERING SUNDAY

Voucher

This voucher can be exchanged for

one full bedroom tidy-up

breakfast in bed

washing up on ...
(and the saucepans!)

other ...

Just to say Thanks, Mum !

Love from

FIFTH SUNDAY OF LENT

Thought for the day

Through Christ's death, full life would come to people of all nations and generations.

Readings

Jeremiah 31:31-34
Psalm 51:1-12 or Psalm 119:9-16
Hebrews 5:5-10
John 12:20-33

Aim

To recognise that Jesus' willingness to give his life is proof of his love for us.

Starter

Forfeits. Sit in a circle and spin a tray in the middle, calling out someone's name. That person tries to catch the tray before it clatters to the ground. If they fail, they have to pay a forfeit. Ideas for forfeits: count from ten (or twenty) back to zero; hop round the outside of the circle; give one of your hairs; blow up a balloon; wear a hat for the rest of the game.

Teaching

One of the helpers (or a primed child) produces a tube of Rolos which has only one sweet left in it. You notice it and beg to have it as you love Rolos. The Rolo owner lays it on thick that this is their pack of Rolos, and they saved up all their pocket money to buy them. It's an awful lot to expect them to give up. Go on begging, reminding them of how nice you are and how much you mean to them. Eventually they say, 'Oh, OK – I suppose you're worth it!' and give you their last Rolo. Everyone else can say, 'Aah!'

Explain that today, the Fifth Sunday in Lent, we're starting to look at what it cost Jesus to do his work as our Saviour. (Place a cross down on the floor in the middle of the circle.) It's one thing to dedicate your life to teaching and healing, wandering around the country with no definite place to stay, and working long hours without pay. Jesus had been doing that for the last two or three years.

But now things were taking a new turn. He knew that it wouldn't be long before his work of loving people to freedom led him straight into trouble, trouble that would be bound to end in giving up his life in a tortured, shaming death on the Roman gallows. (Raise the cross to standing and hold it there.)

Not surprisingly, Jesus shuddered at the thought of having to go through all that. It wouldn't just be the physical pain, either. It would mean taking on himself the whole terrible load of the world's sin and evil, and going on loving and forgiving to the very end. (Cover the cross with a purple cloth.) Everything human in Jesus cried out against having to do that. The cost was so great and so demanding.

But then he remembered that the whole point of him being on earth was that he had come to save the people he loved. And to Jesus we are worth all the suffering. (Uncover the cross.) So today we remember that Jesus was prepared to say, 'Yes!' because he loves us that much.

Praying

My Lord, what love is this,
that pays so dearly,
that I, the guilty one, may go free!
Amazing love, O what sacrifice,
the Son of God given for me.
My debt he pays and my death he dies,
that I might live.

(Taken from the song *Amazing love* by Graham Kendrick © 1989 Make Way Music)

Activities

The sheet can be made into a prayer corner for the next two weeks, to help them think about the cross and begin to understand at a deeper level what it meant for Jesus to give his life to set us free. Encourage them to look up the Bible references for each day and set aside a short time each day to pray the prayer.

Notes

PALM SUNDAY

Thought for the day

As the Messiah, Jesus enters Jerusalem, knowing that he rides towards rejection and death in order to save his people.

Readings

Liturgy of the Palms:
Mark 11:1-11 or John 12:12-16
Psalm 118:1-2, 19-24

Liturgy of the Passion:
Isaiah 50:4-9a
Psalm 31:9-16
Philippians 2:5-11
Mark 14:1-15:47 or Mark 15:1-39 (40-47)

Aim

To understand that Jesus is making a Messianic statement as he enters Jerusalem.

Starter

If possible, let the children join in with the all-age procession, playing their instruments, dancing and singing as they go. Or gather all the age groups and take them on a Palm Sunday procession, preferably outside. Take a portable tape player so they can all sing along with the songs.

Teaching

Bring along a little olive oil and a cloth, a crown, and this notice: 'Anointed as God's chosen one = Messiah (in Hebrew) = Christ (in Greek).'

Put the notice, the olive oil and the crown in the centre, and remind the children of when David was a shepherd boy and God chose him to be the future king. To show he was chosen (choose a volunteering child), David was anointed with olive oil. (Pour a little oil on the volunteer's head and wipe it with the towel, so they understand what being anointed means.) David was God's chosen king, and when he grew up, he became the king of Israel. (Place the crown on the same child's head.)

Long after King David had died, everyone looked back to those wonderful days when he had been their king, and they also looked forward to the time when God would send his anointed, chosen One to be King over all the world for ever. They knew this anointed one would be from King David's family. They called this anointed One the Hebrew for 'anointed' – which is 'Messiah'. We usually call it 'Christ' which is the same thing in Greek, the language the Gospels were written in.

Many, many years later, Jesus was born, of David's family. Gradually people began to realise that this was the Messiah, the son of King David who would reign for ever. When Jesus rode a donkey into Jerusalem, they all got really excited, and cheered and shouted and sang their hearts out. The prophets had even said the Messiah would enter Jerusalem riding on a donkey, and here Jesus was, doing it! 'Hosanna! Hosanna!' they all shouted. 'Hosanna to the Son of King David! Hosanna for the glorious kingdom he's going to bring us!' (One of the leaders can be a donkey and one of the children can ride the donkey while the others all shout their Hosannas and wave their streamers.)

What the people didn't quite understand was that Jesus' kingdom was not like a country on a map, but was a kingdom of love, joy and peace in people's hearts and lives. Jesus is the Christ, the Messiah, and reigns as King in our hearts now, just as he can reign in the hearts of anyone, living anywhere, at any time.

Praying

You are the King of Glory,
you are the Prince of Peace,
you are the Lord of heaven and earth,
you're the Son of righteousness.
Angels bow down before you,
worship and adore,
for you have the words of eternal life,
you are Jesus Christ the Lord.
Hosanna to the Son of David!
Hosanna to the King of kings!
Glory in the highest heaven,
for Jesus the Messiah reigns!

(Mavis Ford
© 1978 Springtide/CopyCare)

Activities

The different strips on the sheet can be mounted on card and fixed together to form the star of David, so that the children sense the drawing together of all the Law and the prophets in Jesus.

> ### Notes

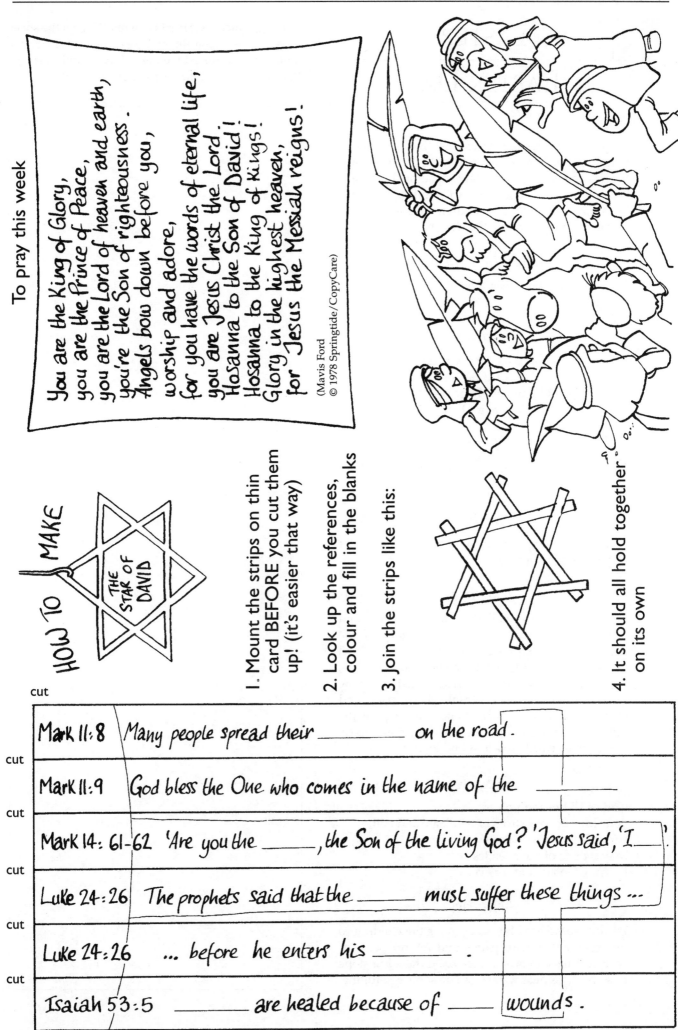

To pray this week

You are the King of Glory,
you are the Prince of Peace,
you are the Lord of heaven and earth,
you're the Son of righteousness.
Angels bow down before you,
worship and adore,
for you have the words of eternal life,
you are Jesus Christ the Lord.
Hosanna to the Son of David!
Hosanna to the King of kings!
Glory in the highest heaven,
for Jesus the Messiah reigns!

(Mavis Ford)
© 1978 Springtide/CopyCare)

HOW TO MAKE

THE STAR OF DAVID

1. Mount the strips on thin card BEFORE you cut them up! (it's easier that way)

2. Look up the references, colour and fill in the blanks

3. Join the strips like this:

4. It should all hold together on its own

cut

Mark 11:8	Many people spread their _____ on the road.
cut	
Mark 11:9	God bless the One who comes in the name of the _____
cut	
Mark 14:61-62	'Are you the _____, the Son of the living God?' Jesus said, 'I___'.
cut	
Luke 24:26	The prophets said that the _____ must suffer these things ...
cut	
Luke 24:26	... before he enters his _____ .
cut	
Isaiah 53:5	_____ are healed because of ___ wounds.

cut

EASTER

EASTER DAY

If possible, it is recommended that the children and young people are in church with the other age groups today. Use and adapt some of the all-age ideas from the *Living Stones* Complete Resource Book, and involve the children in some of the music and in decorating the church.

Thought for the day

Jesus is alive; Love has won the victory over sin and death.

Readings

Acts 10:34-43 or Isaiah 25:6-9
Psalm 118:1-2, 14-24
1 Corinthians 15:1-11 or Acts 10:34-43
John 20:1-18 or Mark 16:1-8

Aim

To sense the amazement, fear and joy of those meeting the risen Jesus.

Starter

A traditional egg hunt is good to have on Easter Day, preferably outside.

Teaching

Beforehand prepare an Easter garden on a tray, and use this as a focus for telling the story of the Resurrection. Follow either the Mark or the John version, according to what is being read in church; in a suitable version it can be read directly from the Bible. In your reading, think about pace and expression, allowing pauses and bringing out the different characters and responses in your voice. Make Jesus' words spacious and loving.

Praying

God of all life and power,
your love proved stronger than hate and evil,
stronger than death itself.
May the life of the risen Jesus
live in us today and for ever.

Activities

Prepare some hard-boiled eggs for the children to decorate, either with paints and felt-tip pens, or with sequins and beads stuck on. If there is a slope or some grass nearby, they can do some egg rolling.

The egg which rolls furthest wins. Also on the sheet there is an explanation of the egg symbolism, and a look at the confused feelings of Jesus' followers on that first day of the Resurrection.

Notes

To pray this week

God of all life and power,
your love proved stronger
than hate and evil,
stronger than death itself.
May the life of the risen Jesus
live in us today – and for ever.

What's happening?

BUT JESUS WAS COMPLETELY
DEAD – HOW CAN HE BE ALIVE?

It seems impossible
but I can see him!

SO THIS IS WHAT JESUS WAS
TRYING TO TELL US!

NOW I
KNOW FOR
CERTAIN THAT
JESUS IS THE SON
OF GOD!

I'm scared!

On the
first Easter
Day people
felt quite
mixed up!
Can you
unscramble what
they were thinking?

If you have a slope or
hill you can roll the eggs
down. The one which goes
furthest is the winner!

Decorate
an egg!

1. Use a hard-
boiled egg

2. Decorate
with paints
or crayons
or felt-tip
pens

Why do
we have eggs
at Easter?

Colour in
all the dotted
bits to see
the answer

SECOND SUNDAY OF EASTER

Thought for the day

Our faith in the risen Christ is bound to affect the way we live.

Readings

Acts 4:32-35
Psalm 133
1 John 1:1–2:2
John 20:19-31

Aim

To know the story of Jesus appearing to the disciples and helping Thomas.

Starter

Try again. Stand in a circle with one person in the centre. They throw a beanbag or soft ball to each person in turn. If someone misses a catch, they are given a second chance (or as many as it takes!).

Teaching

Sometimes we are given just one chance to get something right, and if we mess it up that time, there are no second chances. Share some examples, such as music exams, writing in ink rather than pencil, answering a question on a quiz show, converting a try, or entering a colouring competition. Sometimes we feel like kicking ourselves afterwards and would love to put the clock back, so we could do it again, but differently.

Today we're going to hear about someone who missed out, but was given a second chance.

Have everyone (apart from one who is going to be Thomas) sitting on chairs, and one extra chair left free. Have an unlit candle in the centre. Remind them about Jesus rising from death on the first Easter Day, and explain that he came to where the disciples were gathered on that Sunday evening. They had locked the door because they were scared. (Rattle a bunch of keys.) As they can see, one place is empty. That's Thomas's place, and for some reason, which we don't know, Thomas wasn't there that evening. Perhaps he was so upset about Jesus dying that he wanted to be by himself.

Suddenly (light the candle) there was Jesus in the room with them. Once they'd got over their fear and astonishment, they were all very happy to see him, real and alive! Then Jesus left them just as quietly as he had come. (Blow out the candle.) But what about Thomas?

Well, during the week the disciples told Thomas what had happened, and Thomas couldn't really believe it. It was just too good to be true. And he said, 'Unless I see him with my own eyes, and touch his wounds, I refuse to believe it.'

A week later, the disciples are all together again, and this time Thomas is there as well. Once again Jesus suddenly appeared among them, without a fuss – he was just there! (Light the candle.) And because Jesus understood what Thomas had been going through, he went straight to him. 'Here I am, Thomas,' he said. 'Here are the wounds in my hands and side and feet. It's really me! Do you want to touch my wounds to make sure?'

Thomas didn't need that kind of proof any more. The experience of Jesus' presence was good enough – now, he *knew* it was true, and Jesus really was risen from the dead.

Praying

Dear Jesus,
when Thomas had his questions and his doubts
you met him and helped him to see the truth.
We pray for all those who have questions and doubts.
May they soon discover how real you are. Amen.

Activities

On the sheet there is a dot-to-dot to discover a hidden picture, and various examples of camouflage, where something is there but we don't see it straightaway. The children will each need a piece of tracing paper or greaseproof paper and some plain paper to make the 'discovering truth' model.

Notes

To pray this week

Dear Jesus,
when Thomas had his questions and his doubts you met him and helped him to see the truth.
We pray for all those who have questions and doubts.
May they soon discover how real you are. – Amen –

Can you spot the camouflaged creatures?
They're there, but we don't see them straight-away

DISCOVER THE TRUTH

Trace this onto tracing paper

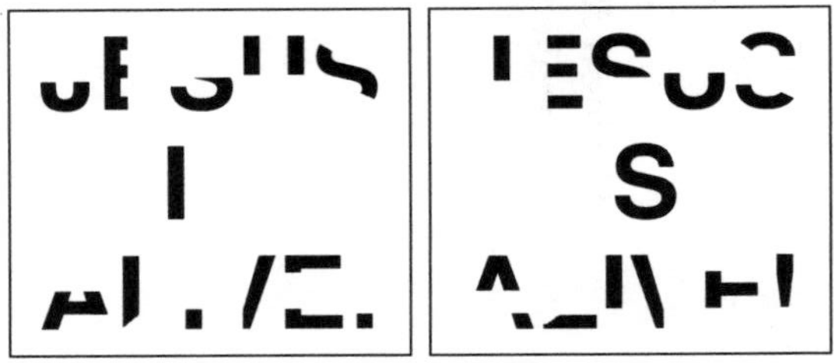

THIRD SUNDAY OF EASTER

Thought for the day

Having redeemed us by his death, Jesus can offer us the forgiveness of our sin, which sets us free to live.

Readings

Acts 3:12-19
Psalm 4
1 John 3:1-7
Luke 24:36b-48

Aim

To know today's Gospel, and the importance of repentance and forgiveness.

Starter

Take the children on a scary 'lion hunt'.

Teaching

For the teaching today, write out the separate speeches, and give them to different people to say during the telling of the story. These are:

- Jesus: 'Peace be with you!'

- Various disciples: 'Help! It must be a ghost!' 'Aah!' 'A g-g-ghost!'

- Jesus: 'Why are you so scared? I'm not a ghost! Look at my hands and my feet. It's me, Jesus! Touch me if you like. You can see I have a living body. A ghost does not have a body like this!'

- Various disciples: 'Oh Jesus, you're alive!' 'Yes, I can see you are real. That's incredible!' 'Yippee! Jesus is alive!'

- All together: 'Are you REALLY alive, Jesus? It seems too good to be true!'

- Jesus: 'Do you have any food here?'

- One disciple: 'Yes, there's some cooked fish. Here you are.'

- Jesus: 'Thanks!'

- Various disciples (whisper): 'Look, he's eating.' 'Ghosts don't eat normal food!' 'He MUST be alive!'

Give out the speeches and imagine you are all in the room where Jesus came. Narrate the events, with the characters reading their parts. Then go on to tell them how Jesus helped them understand what had been happening. Hold a Bible and flick through the Old Testament as you explain that he took them through all the things that had been written about him in the prophets and the Psalms.

- Jesus: 'It is written that the Christ would be killed and rise from death on the third day. You saw these things happen – you are witnesses.'

- Various disciples: 'Yes, that's true, we saw it all happen.' 'Yes, we did.' 'We know it's true.'

- Jesus: 'You must tell people to change their hearts and lives. If they do this, their sins will be forgiven.'

- One disciple: 'OK, Jesus, we'll tell them. Where do we start?'

- Jesus: 'You must start in Jerusalem and then preach these things in my name to all nations.'

Pray together for all the people who will only hear about Jesus' forgiveness because we tell them during our lifetimes.

Praying

Dear Jesus, when we are scared you make us brave,
when we are worried you calm us down,
and when we are listening you tell us what to do.
Help us to listen well and tell others about you,
so they can enjoy your friendship as well.

Activities

The sheet can be turned into a pop-up picture, where Jesus suddenly stands among his friends. They are helped to see that Jesus comes among us in person as we worship together.

Notes

PEACE BE WITH YOU!

Make this
POP-UP PICTURE
of Luke 24:36b–48

1. Colour the picture
2. Fold the lines as shown (a)
3. Put a paper clip to hold the hidden bit of the picture (b)
4. As you say 'Jesus himself stood among them and said ...' pull the sides, so the paper clip pops off and Jesus is there

(a)   (b)

To pray this week

Dear Jesus, when we are scared
you make us brave,
when we are worried
you calm us down,
and when we are listening
you tell us what to do.
Help us to listen well
and tell others about you,
so they can enjoy your
friendship as well.

The Lord is here!

Jesus comes among us in person as we worship
Jesus comes among us in person as we worship

FOURTH SUNDAY OF EASTER

Thought for the day

'I am the Good Shepherd and I lay down my life for the sheep.'

Readings

Acts 4:5-12
Psalm 23
1 John 3:16-24
John 10:11-18

Aim

To look at what it means for Jesus to be the Good Shepherd.

Starter

To the rescue! Firefighters, lifeboat crews and mountain rescue teams are all willing to drop what they're doing and race to the rescue. At one corner of the room have a hose pipe, at another have a length of rope (or a washing line), and at another a blow-up ring on a length of string. Everyone walks about in the space in the middle of the room until one of three alarms is sounded. If it's a bell they race to the sea rescue, and all line up holding the string, hauling the ring in. If it's a whistle they race to the mountain rescue, and all line up and walk along a pretend narrow ledge, holding the rope. If it's a 'nee-nor' siren (just voicing it is fine) they race to the fire rescue, and line up to hold the hose, directing it at the flames.

Teaching

It takes courage to join any of those rescue teams, and those who do it know that they may be putting themselves at risk, but they are willing to do it so that others will be saved.

It was a risky, dangerous business for Jesus to rescue the human race, using only the power of love. In today's Gospel Jesus talks about himself as the Good Shepherd, who is willing even to lay down his life for the sheep. We're going to look at what it means to be a good shepherd, so that we can better understand what Jesus meant.

Have most of the children as sheep, some as wolves and bears, one as a hired shepherd, who's only doing it for the money, and one as a good shepherd who loves the sheep. Talk the sheep through their life on the hillside, with the good shepherd watching that they don't get lost, finding them tasty pastures full of wet, juicy grass to munch, leading them to drink at the water, and getting them safely into a pen (made of chairs) for the night. The shepherd lies down in the doorway to sleep. Meanwhile the wolves and bears stand back, howling and waiting for a chance to catch a sheep. If they start to come near, the shepherd throws crumpled paper 'stones' at them and that frightens them off.

Stop the action and swap shepherds. This shepherd reads the newspaper instead of checking that the sheep have enough to eat and drink, and he's listening to his personal stereo so he can't hear the sheep bleating when they're frightened. If a wolf comes near, he might throw a stone or two, but the wolves know that it's worth waiting, as he'll soon lose interest. When he gets deep into his *Goosebumps* book, some of the wolves creep nearer and are just about to grab a sheep. The shepherd sees the wolves and runs away! That kind of shepherd is no good for the sheep. That kind of leader is no good for God's people.

So when Jesus says that he is the Good Shepherd, we know what he means – that he loves us and looks after us, even if it turns difficult and dangerous; even if it costs him his life.

Praying

Jesus, we thank you that you were willing
even to lay down your life for us.
May the love which saved us
live in us every day and for ever.
Amen.

Activities

There is a picture of the sheep about to be attacked by the wolves, with the hired shepherd running away. They draw in the good shepherd coming to the rescue. There is also a cost-counting activity and it includes Jesus going through with our rescue, even though he knew it would cost him his life.

Notes

FIFTH SUNDAY OF EASTER

Thought for the day

To produce fruit we need to be joined on to the true vine.

Readings

Acts 8:26-40
Psalm 22:25-31
1 John 4:7-21
John 15:1-8

Aim

To look at the importance of our being joined on to the true vine, if we are hoping to produce fruit.

Starter

Grow a vine. As children come in, tie a length of green string or wool round their waist, so it hangs down the back like a tail. Leave one child (or a leader) with no string and sit that person on a chair. When everyone is ready, explain that they are going to make themselves into a grapevine, using all the children. It has to start from the person on the chair, who has two hands free, and they have to obey this rule: one string to one hand. (It's good training for children to practise organising themselves like this, sometimes. Don't interfere unless it's really necessary and let them work through the mistakes to the solution.) Give out grapes to everyone when they're ready.

Teaching

Bring along (or take them outside to see) a growing plant. Notice how its branches have grown, rather like we grew our 'grapevine', and notice any buds or flowers which are the first signs of fruit. Also look at an off-cut from the plant. Will this piece be able to flower and fruit like the other branches? No, it won't. Why not? Talk together about how the branches and stems carry all the goodness, and without being joined on to the living plant, with its strong roots, the cut-off branch dies.

Have a grapevine outline drawn on a large sheet of paper. Now, from a suitable translation of the Bible, read today's Gospel, where Jesus talks of himself as the true vine, and the importance of us being joined to him if we are going to produce fruit. Talk over what Jesus means, and what kind of fruit we are hoping to produce. As different ideas are given, stick clusters of grapes on to the drawn vine, labelling them. (They may well link up with the ones Paul describes in Galatians 5:22.)

Praying

Jesus, I know I can only produce good fruit
if I'm connected to you, the true vine.
Let your life flow into me and through me
so together we can make a huge harvest!
Amen.

Activities

Using the pictures and instructions on the sheet the children will be making a grapevine. Each child will also need pipe cleaners and green paint.

Notes

I AM THE TRUE VINE

MAKE A GRAPEVINE

You will need

Pipe cleaners for branches

Square of card for the base

Paper clips to fix grapes and leaves on

1. Twist 4 pipe cleaners together and spread the ends out. Tape these to the cardboard base like this:

2. Join on other branches by twisting the pipe cleaners together

3. Colour the grapes and leaves. Fix them on the vine with paper clips

4. Clip on the leaves and fruit

To pray this week

Jesus, I know I can only produce good fruit if I'm connected to you, the true vine. Let your life flow into me and through me so together we can make a huge harvest! — Amen —

Fold this flap and stick on to the base.

How can we be joined on branches?

B

L T T G

S N T

J

U L V S

R

S

U

O

E

N

Y

I

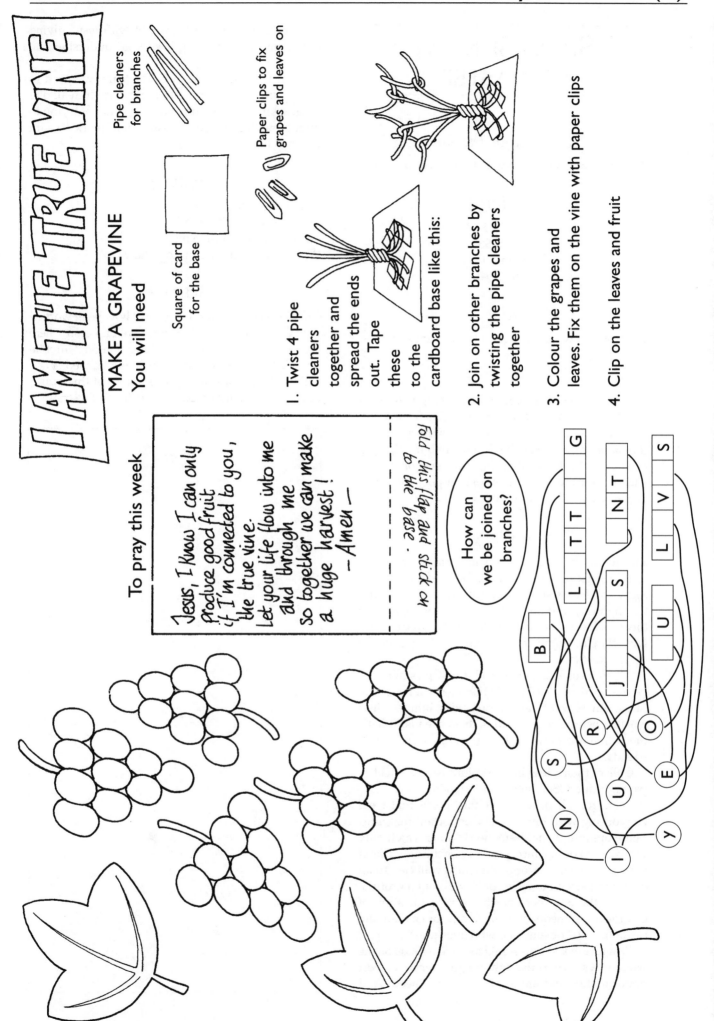

Sixth Sunday of Easter

Thought for the day

We are to love one another as Jesus loves us.

Readings

Acts 10:44-48
Psalm 98
1 John 5:1-6
John 15:9-17

Aim

To know that we are not servants but friends of Jesus.

Starter

Do this, do that! The captain of the ship is given a suitable hat to wear, and everyone else is the crew, obeying the orders to make the ship sail well. (Possible orders: scrub the decks; climb the rigging; hoist the sail; lower the sail; drop anchor; weigh anchor; coil the ropes; everyone to port; everyone to starboard; all hands on deck.)

Teaching

Talk about jobs where it's very important that people just do what they're told, and obey orders straight-away (such as soldiers and sailors, astronauts and fire fighters, and those working in an operating theatre). It doesn't matter whether they understand why they're doing it – as long as the person in charge knows.

When Jesus was talking to his disciples not long before he died, he told them that he wasn't going to call them servants any more, with him as their master. Instead he was calling them friends. What's the difference between being servants and being friends?

Collect their ideas in two columns on a sheet of paper, headed 'Servants' and 'Friends'.

Being friends of Jesus like this means that we'll be working with him on very important missions. There are things that Jesus needs done which only we can do! For instance, you may be the only friend of Jesus available to work with him in your classroom on your particular table, or in your playground. You are the only person who is right for a job of comforting someone in your family, or challenging the behaviour of someone who lives nearby.

Whatever jobs Jesus wants to work with us on, he will always give us the right training for it, the best opportunities and any special help we need. And we'll be working as a team, not with Jesus giving orders and us just doing it without understanding why.

So, if we want to be in God's team, we need to make sure we're keeping in touch with him all day long, asking his opinion and help, and not trying to go it alone. Jesus doesn't want us to work *for* him but *with* him.

Praying

Here I am, Jesus,
ready to work with you
for the coming of the kingdom.
What's our next mission together?

Activities

On the sheet is a cartoon version of how Peter worked with God on the Cornelius household mission. There are also instructions for making a model mobile phone, to which today's prayer is attached. Each child will need a suitably sized piece of thick card, or card box such as tablets come in, and a straw.

Notes

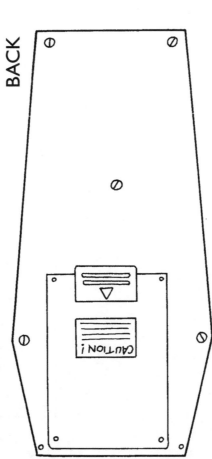

Make a model mobile!

You will need:

an empty thin box (such as for tablets)

or an individual drink carton

a straw

What you do:

1. Colour the front and back of the mobile, and cut out
2. Make a hole in the box and poke in the straw
3. Stick the pictures on the front and back of the box

ASCENSION DAY

Thought for the day

Having bought back our freedom with the giving of his life, Jesus enters into the full glory to which he is entitled.

Readings

Acts 1:1-11 or Daniel 7:9-14
Psalm 47 or Psalm 93
Ephesians 1:15-23 or Acts 1:1-11
Luke 24:44-53

Activities

It is likely that Ascension Day services for schools will not need a separate programme for children and young people. Children in church can work on this drawing and colouring activity during the sermon.

Fold and stick backs together

Jesus, the Saviour, was born

The angel Gabriel told Mary she would have a baby, the Son of God

Make a Jesus book

Colour the pictures

Stick on to inside of back cover

Jesus rose from the dead

THE EARTHLY LIFE OF JESUS

Cover pages: fold, don't stick

Jesus ascended into heaven

Fold and stick backs together

Jesus was crucified and died for us

Jesus went about healing and teaching

Seventh Sunday of Easter

Thought for the day

Although now hidden from our sight, Jesus lives for ever, and in him we can live the Resurrection life even while we are on earth.

Readings

Acts 1:15-17, 21-26
Psalm 1
1 John 5:9-13
John 17:6-19

Aim

To know what the disciples did about replacing Judas.

Starter

Tell everyone what the forfeit is for whoever draws the short straw. (For example, walk backwards to the window; hop around the circle; catch a ball thrown to you three times running.) Have as many straws as there are children in the group, and cut one of the straws short. Hold them so that only the ends show, and everyone takes one. Whoever has the short straw has to do the forfeit.

Teaching

If the children have missed out on Ascension Day, go over what happened in more detail. Otherwise refer them to the Ascension and explain what the disciples did when they got back to Jerusalem. They met up and prayed together, waiting as Jesus had told them to, so they would be ready for the coming of the Holy Spirit.

And they had a job to do, before that happened. How many apostles had Jesus chosen? Twelve. How many were there now? (Say the names of the apostles slowly, so they can count. The list is given in Acts 1:13.) Who was missing? Judas. Why? Because he was the one who had betrayed Jesus to the Roman guards, and had later killed himself.

What the disciples had to do was to replace the missing apostle, so that they would once again be twelve. Give the children cards with their own words on, written large and clearly.

Peter   Listen, everyone. Judas was one of us, and he is no longer with us. We must choose someone to take his place.

James   Must it be someone who was with Jesus all the time, like we were?

Peter: Yes, it must.

John   What about Justus? He is a good person.

Peter   Right. Any other ideas?

Andrew   What about Matthias? He is a good person, too.

Philip   And they have both been with Jesus all the time.

John   I wonder which person God thinks is best for this job?

Andrew   Let's pray, and ask him.

Peter   Yes, let's all pray. Lord, you know what everyone is like. Show us which of these two you have chosen. Thank you, Lord. Amen.

Explain that when they had prayed, they pulled straws, like we did in our game, and the one who drew the short straw was Matthias. So Matthias became the twelfth disciple.

Praying

Lord, please show me
the way you want me to live.
Train me to think like you think,
see as you see,
and love as you love. Amen.

Activities

On the sheet there is a pyramid to make up and use as a 3D checklist for making decisions God's way. They are also told about Jesus praying for us to keep us safe while we are in the world doing God's work.

Notes

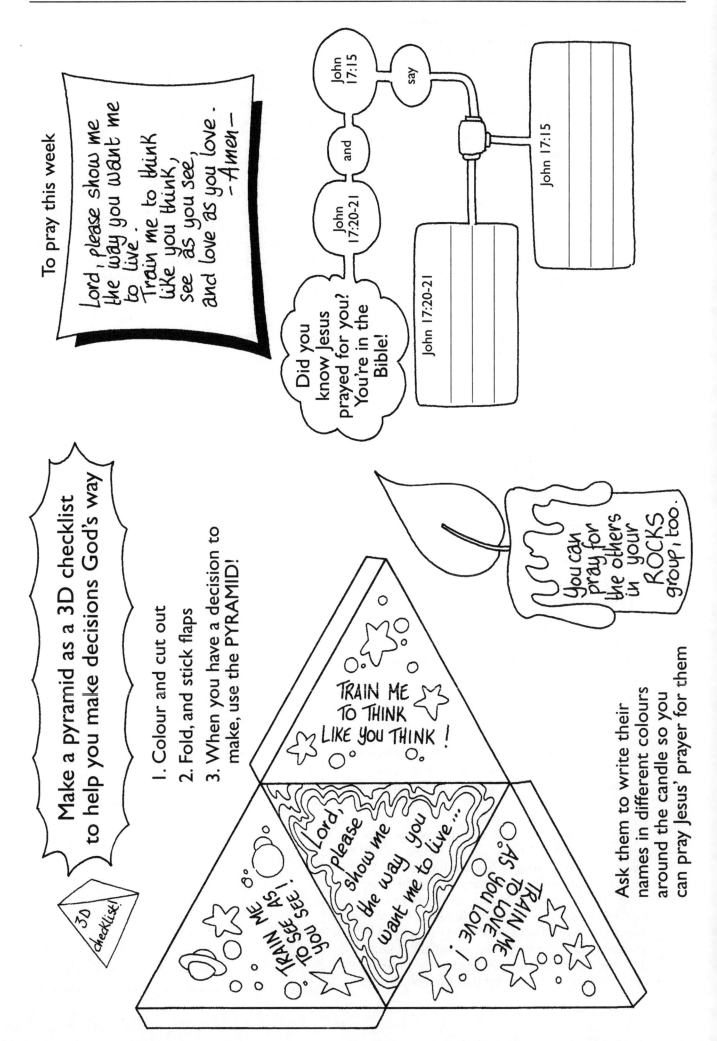

To pray this week

Lord, please show me the way you want me to live.
Train me to think like you think,
see as you see,
and love as you love.
— Amen —

Did you know Jesus prayed for you? You're in the Bible!

John 17:15

say

John 17:20-21

and

John 17:20-21

John 17:15

Make a pyramid as a 3D checklist to help you make decisions God's way

1. Colour and cut out
2. Fold, and stick flaps
3. When you have a decision to make, use the PYRAMID!

3D checklist

TRAIN ME TO THINK LIKE YOU THINK!

Lord, please show me the way you want me to live...

TRAIN ME TO SEE AS YOU SEE!

TRAIN ME TO LOVE AS YOU LOVE!

You can pray for the others in your ROCKS group, too.

Ask them to write their names in different colours around the candle so you can pray Jesus' prayer for them

PENTECOST

Thought for the day

The Holy Spirit of God is poured out in power on the expectant disciples, just as Jesus promised.

Readings

Acts 2:1-21 or Ezekiel 37:1-14
Psalm 104:24-34, 35b
Romans 8:22-27 or Acts 2:1-21
John 15:26-27; 16:4b-15

Aim

To know the events of Pentecost.

Starter

Give each child a different coloured bunch of wool lengths. (For larger numbers of children make several groups.) With the bunch of wool provide a written message, reading it out to the child as you give it, and checking they know what it says. Now they all go round giving their message, and one length of their wool, to every other child. Here are the messages:

1. The disciples were waiting and praying.

2. Pentecost means fifty days after Passover.

3. Jesus had promised to send the Holy Spirit.

4. The Spirit sounded like a rushing wind.

5. The Spirit looked like flames of fire.

(Add to these or prune them as necessary for your group.)

Teaching

Everyone should now have a bunch of different coloured wools. They lay these out in front of them. The children can now help you tell the story of Pentecost, by remembering the messages which went with each colour of wool.

Once everyone has added the bits of the story, pull it all together by reading the events as told direct from Acts, using a suitable translation. We have all been working together to tell the story today, and the Holy Spirit empowers us to work together with God and one another for good every day of our lives. What a lot of good can happen by seventy years' time if all of us, and all the children in all the other Rocks groups, work in the power of the Holy Spirit every day for the rest of our lives!

Praying

Come, Holy Spirit of God,
come to me and fill my life.
Let me live in your strength from now on,
and work with you
so that great good gets done!

Activities

The children can make flame crowns from their sheets. Provide flame-size pieces of shiny red or orange paper to add to their coloured flames, and staple them to the rim. They are also encouraged to think of a quiet space during the day at home where they can get in touch with God each day, and pray the week's prayer.

Notes

A

COME, HOLY SPIRIT !

cut

Stick to **A**

Make this into a long strip to fit round your head

Make these flames bright and sparkly, cut them out and stick them on the crown

HOLY SPIRIT

Pray this each day of the week

Come, Holy Spirit of God, come to me and fill my life. Let me live in Your strength from now on, and work with you so that great good gets done !

If you haven't got a desert island, find a quiet space where you can get in touch with God each day at home. Here are some ideas —

ORDINARY TIME

TRINITY SUNDAY

Thought for the day

The mysterious and holy nature of the one true God is beyond our understanding, but it is both communal harmony and individual personality, Father, Son and Holy Spirit.

Readings

Isaiah 6:1-8
Psalm 29
Romans 8:12-17
John 3:1-17

Aim

To be introduced to God as Father, Son and Spirit.

Starter

Bring in a lot of tight rolls of newspaper, thick enough to be firm. Work together to make them into an Eiffel Tower, using sticky tape to join the rolls together. They should find that the strongest shape to use is a triangle. If they aren't getting beyond the bendy stage, you can subtly suggest the use of triangles!

Teaching

Draw their attention to the way triangles hold firm, and look at one to see why this is. All the way round, two hold the third in place.

Explain that today the whole Church is taking a look at what God is really like, and worshipping him. What do we know about God already? For a start, how many Gods are there? They may well mention lots of gods they have heard of. Agree that people through history have invented lots of gods, and anything we worship – including football stars and fashion – can be made into a kind of god by us. But we know that all these are pretend gods, which we make or think of ourselves.

There is only one true God and nobody invented God – God was already there; he always has been and always will be. That makes the one true God the only one worthy of our worship. And that's why we and our families make the effort to get up on a Sunday; we know that God is real and we come to worship him.

What is the only true God like? God is Father, the Creator (write 'Father' across the triangle), Son, our Saviour (write 'Jesus' in the same place), and Holy Spirit (write 'Holy Spirit' in the same place). We can't see the words clearly now because they are all one, and that's what God is like. If we also write the character of God round the edges (do this) we can see that the whole 'shape' of God is Father, Son and Holy Spirit all supporting and including each other.

That's why we call God a Trinity, or Tri-Unity – tri = 3 and unity = 1.

Praying

Glory be to the Father
and to the Son
and to the Holy Spirit,
as God WAS in the beginning
IS now
and SHALL BE for ever. Amen.

Activities

Using the sheet the children can make a hand-held creed. Each child will need a paper fastener for this. They can also build up a collage picture of God, using the qualities and characteristics named. For this the group will need a large sheet of coloured paper, and the words can be stuck all over it, together with pictures which match up with the descriptions. When planning, look at the words and bring pictures which you feel are appropriate, for the children to choose from.

Notes

72

PROPER 4

Sunday between 29 May and 4 June inclusive
(if after Trinity Sunday)

Thought for the day

Jesus has the words of eternal life – he sheds light on a right attitude to the Law.

Readings

1 Samuel 3:1-10 (11-20) or Deuteronomy 5:12-15
Psalm 139:1-6, 13-18 or Psalm 81:1-10
2 Corinthians 4:5-12
Mark 2:23-3:6

Aim

To know the story of Jesus healing the man with the withered arm.

Starter

Give out soft balls, beanbags or rolled socks to each pair of children and ask them to practise throwing and catching to each other using only one hand at a time.

Teaching

Share how you all got on. It's hard to catch one-handed and it takes lots of practice. Today we're going to hear about a man who had to live one-handed because one of his arms didn't work.

We don't know his name. We do know that he had come to worship at the synagogue on the Sabbath with all the other Jewish people in his town. Remind them that Jewish people always worship on the Sabbath, which means seventh day because of what God did on the seventh day of creation. (What did God do that day? Nothing! Having made the whole of the heavens and the earth, he rested on the seventh day, and so the people kept it holy, doing no work on it and worshipping God who had made every-thing so well.) So the Sabbath was *No Work* day, and we need to remember that because it's important in our story.

It so happened that Jesus was visiting their syna-gogue that Sabbath, and he noticed this man with his arm all shrunk and withered so he couldn't use it. Jesus saw how difficult it was for the man to manage like this, and, being Jesus, he felt very sorry for him. More than anything, he wanted to make the man's life easier; he wanted his arm to work as well as anyone else's.

Now, a few big questions . . .

- What day was it? (The Sabbath.)

- What was the rule about the Sabbath? (It's a *No Work* day.)
- Would it be work for Jesus to make the man better? (Take a vote on it.)
- So would it be right or wrong for Jesus to make the man better? (Take a vote on it.)

Now the teachers of the Law were hoping to catch Jesus doing something wrong, but they were finding that very difficult, because he never did! But this gave them something to pounce on. They pointed out that this was the Sabbath, and no work should be done on it. They were saying it would be breaking the Law for Jesus to heal the man.

So what would Jesus, the Lord of Love, think about that? (Collect their ideas.)

In fact, Jesus was angry at the teachers of the Law because they were so determined to keep the Law that they had stopped doing loving things like feeling sorry for a man with a useless arm, and wanting to make him better.

Jesus decided that the loving way of healing was keeping God's Law much more than sticking to picky detailed rules which shut love out. So he told the man to stretch out his poor withered arm, and, with all his healing love, he made that arm grow into a strong useful one again!

More questions . . .

- What do you think the man thought about Jesus healing him on the Sabbath? (Share ideas.)
- What do you think the teachers of the Law thought about it? (Share ideas.)

All the people were very happy that Jesus used the Sabbath to do great good, but the teachers were very offended.

Praying

Give me a loving heart, Jesus,
so that I want to help people
as you helped the man.
Make me brave enough
to go on loving and caring
even if people think I'm mad.
Amen.

Activities

On the sheet the Law of love has got cluttered with lots of extra rules. They can clear these away to reveal the real spirit of God's Law. Also there is a ruler to make, with God's love to measure our thinking by. Each child will need a strip of card for this.

Measure your thoughts, words and actions by this:

LOVE GOD and LOVE ONE ANOTHER

1. Cut round the whole shape and turn it over

2. Scribble all over the back of the shape

3. Cut down the lines as shown

4. Fold all the clutter over until the real Law of love is hidden

To pray this week

Give me a loving heart, Jesus,
So that I want to help people
as you helped the man.
Make me brave enough
to go on loving and caring
even if people think I'm mad.
—Amen—

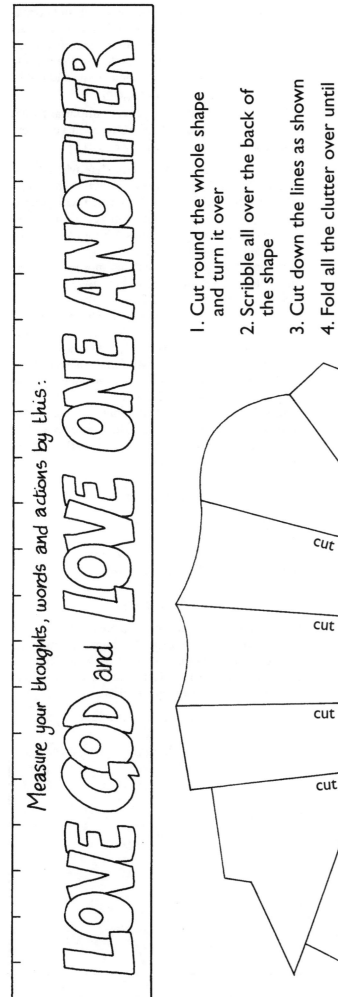

LOVE GOD AND LOVE ONE ANOTHER

cut

PROPER 5

Sunday between 5 and 11 June inclusive
(if after Trinity Sunday)

Thought for the day

Anyone who does God's will is considered a close family member of Jesus.

Readings

1 Samuel 8:4-11 (12-15) 16-20 (11:14-15)
or Genesis 3:8-15
Psalm 138 or Psalm 130
2 Corinthians 4:13-5:1
Mark 3:20-35

Aim

To look at why Jesus' family were worried about him, and what Jesus means by his remark about who is 'family'.

Starter

Play happy families. Give out the cards equally. The children go round swapping cards until they end up with complete family sets. (You can either give a time limit or continue till all sets are complete.)

Teaching

The people in our own families are special to us. Sometimes we have good times together, sometimes the people in our families make us cross and we make them cross. But people in a family are bound together closely because we are physically related to each other. We often look alike and family members will usually stick up for one another, even if we don't always get along easily. In our story today we are going to meet some people in Jesus' family, at a tricky family meeting.

First, let's meet the family. (Give out speech bubbles to various children to read in turn.)

Mary — Hello, I'm Mary. My oldest son is called Jesus. I'm very worried about him.

(Hold up a sign for all the children to read)

All — Why are you worried about Jesus, Mary?

Mary — Well, there are such big crowds of people with him all the time. Some of them have evil spirits. He makes them better, but some people say he's mad.

Jesus' brothers — We are Jesus' brothers. We want to come and take Jesus home with us. It isn't safe to live like he is.

Jesus' sisters — We are Jesus' sisters. It isn't normal to go round healing and teaching great crowds of people. He doesn't even have time to eat! We want to tell Jesus to come home and just be our brother again.

All — But Jesus has very important work to do while he is on earth, you know.

Brothers — But we are his FAMILY!

Thank the readers and explain that when Jesus' mother, brothers and sisters arrived at the house where Jesus was, they found it packed with people, all listening to Jesus. They couldn't get near him, so they told one of Jesus' disciples that they were there, and asked them to tell Jesus.

When Jesus was told that his mother, brothers and sisters had come to take him away home, he looked around at all the faces of the crowd. He could see that they all needed him. He knew he had important work to do with lots of people, and couldn't just live with his family. 'Do you know,' he said, 'who my family is? My family isn't just my mother, brothers and sisters, but every single person who is trying to live God's way.'

Jesus' family had to learn that although Jesus belonged to them in one way, he also belonged to everyone, because his work was to gather lots of people into the family of God.

Praying

Jesus, thank you for letting us
be part of your family.
We hope the family grows and grows
until everyone is living God's way.

Activities

On the sheet there is a pop-up model to make of Jesus in the house with all his huge 'family', and they can draw themselves in it as well. They are also helped to see how Jesus' family extends right over the world and the generations.

Notes

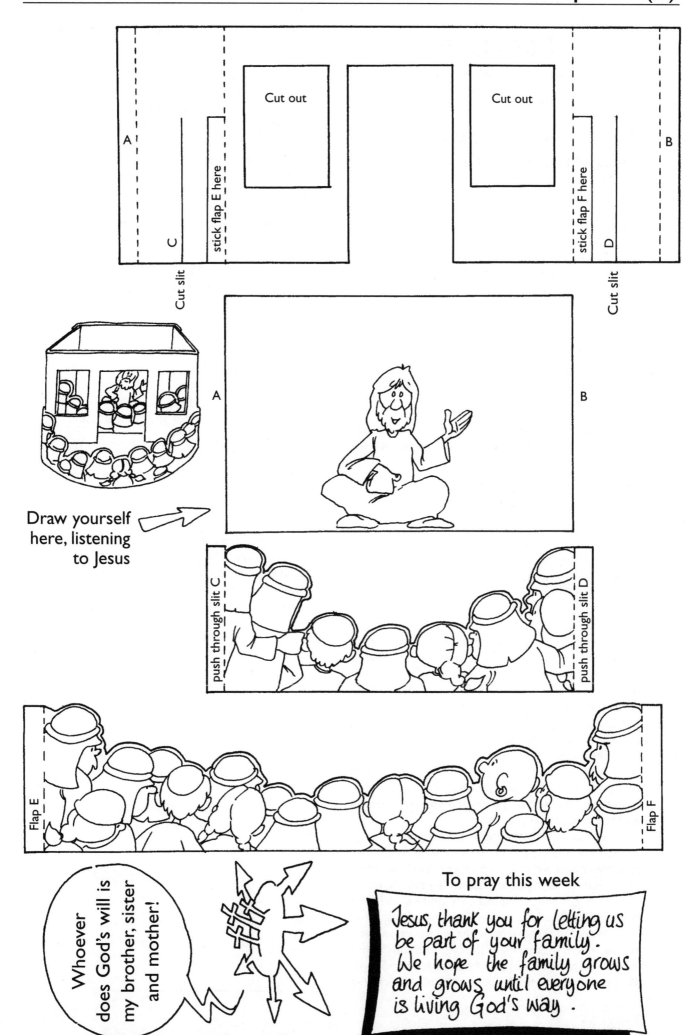

PROPER 6

Thought for the day

From small beginnings, and by God's power, the kingdom of heaven grows.

Readings

1 Samuel 15:34-16:13 or Ezekiel 17:22-24
Psalm 20 or Psalm 92:1-4, 12-15
2 Corinthians 5:6-10 (11-13) 14-17
Mark 4:26-34

Aim

To know the parables of the growing seed and the mustard seed.

Starter

Bring a variety of leaves and have some reference books available so that they can be identified, together with their 'seeds'.

Teaching

Talk about what has been discovered in the opening activity, and how small seeds grow into huge plants. Jesus loved using the world around us to help us understand spiritual things, and today we're going to hear how Jesus used growing seeds to explain spiritual truths for us.

First, he looked at the way seeds grow. (As you speak get a flower pot, fill it with earth and plant a seed in it.) Gardeners will talk about growing vegetables and flowers, but what do they actually do? They get the seeds and they put them in the earth. Then what happens? They water them and put them in a suitable place. Then what? Do they have to sit and watch all the time? Is it no more TV until the vegetables are ready? No, the seeds just grow, more or less on their own! They don't need the gardener to be there fussing over them every minute of the day. Wild plants don't have gardeners and they still manage to grow.

Jesus says that the kingdom of heaven grows rather like that. Just as we can look back and remember that we've grown taller over the last few years, and our knowledge of maths has grown, we've also been growing spiritually. We understand a bit more about who Jesus is now; we are getting more used to talking things over with God in our prayers; we are able to ask some of the big questions about what God is like and how the miracles happened. We are starting to think about what happens when

people die, about right and wrong, about what it costs to be a follower of Jesus.

All this proves that the kingdom of God is growing in you, just as seeds grow in the earth. All that growing is God's doing.

There's another thing about seeds. They start off so small and can end up a huge plant. Jesus noticed that the mustard seed is specially good at that – it's one of the tiniest seeds (show some) and yet it can grow to the size of a tree, with lots of big, spreading branches where the birds love to come and shelter.

He said that the kingdom of heaven grows rather like a mustard seed. Explain that you're not going to tell them what that meant. What do they think he meant by that? (Talk over their ideas. The value of Jesus' parables was to get people thinking for themselves, rather than giving out the answers straightaway.)

Praying

Our Father in heaven,
let your kingdom come.
Let it come in me and my family.
Let it come in my school and my church.
All over the world, Father,
let your kingdom come.

(*Jesus, reign in me* can also be sung as a prayer today.)

Activities

Today's teaching can be read in a picture story on the sheet, and there is a map to plot and colour in the gradual spreading of the kingdom from Jerusalem outwards across the Roman world.

Notes

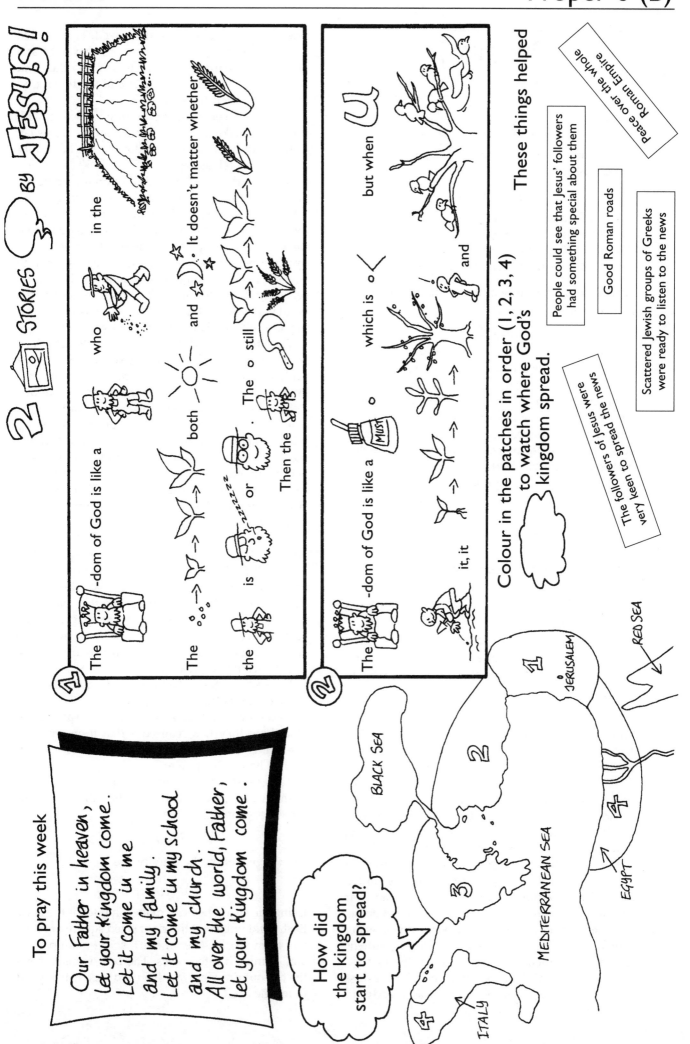

2 STORIES by JESUS!

1 The -dom of God is like a [image] who [image] in the [image]

The [image] both [image] and ☆ ☆. It doesn't matter whether

The [image] is [image] or [image]. The [image] still [image]

Then the [image]

2 The -dom of God is like a [image] which is [image]

The [image] it, it [image] but when [image] and [image]

Colour in the patches in order (1, 2, 3, 4) to watch where God's kingdom spread.

These things helped

People could see that Jesus' followers had something special about them

Good Roman roads

Scattered Jewish groups of Greeks were ready to listen to the news

peace over the whole Roman Empire

The followers of Jesus were very keen to spread the news

To pray this week

Our Father in heaven,
let your kingdom come.
Let it come in me
and my family.
Let it come in my school
and my church.
All over the world, Father,
let your kingdom come.

How did the kingdom start to spread?

BLACK SEA

MEDITERRANEAN SEA

ITALY

JERUSALEM

RED SEA

EGYPT

PROPER 7

Sunday between 19 and 25 June inclusive (if after Trinity Sunday)

Thought for the day

What kind of person is this? Even the wind and waves obey him.

Readings

1 Samuel 17:(1a, 4-11, 19-23) 32-49 or
1 Samuel 17:57-18:5, 10-16 or Job 38:1-11
Psalm 9:9-20 or Psalm 133 or Psalm 107:1-3, 23-32
2 Corinthians 6:1-13; Mark 4:35-41

Aim: To know the story of the calming of the wind and waves.

Starter

Sit everyone in a circle on chairs. You are going to create a storm with actions and sounds. Each 'round', the leader starts off a new action, the person on the right joins in and so on around the circle. When it gets to the leader again, a new action is started. It's important that people carry on with the previous action until the person next to them changes – that makes for a gradual build-up instead of a sudden change. Here are the 'rounds':

1. Flick fingers, so they brush against one another (both hands at once).
2. Tap lightly with two fingers on the palm of other hand.
3. Clap lightly with fingers on palm.
4. Clap fast and louder.
5. Slap thighs with hands – left hand, right hand alternately and quickly.
6. Stamp with feet on the floor.
7. Still stamping, clap while you make wind noises.

(Then work your way back through the numbers to a calm.)

Teaching

Our story today is about a sudden storm, rather like the one we've just made, so we're well practised for providing all the sound effects for it.

Last week we heard a couple of the stories Jesus told – about mustard growing from a tiny seed into a wide spreading tree. Well, Jesus had spent all day out in the open air telling those stories, and teaching and healing people. He used to sit in one of the boats to talk, with the water lapping * the odd fly buzzing around * and all the crowds sitting quietly on the beach. That way they could all see Jesus and hear him, and he could see them. But now it was evening, and there was Jesus sitting in the boat with the water lapping * and he was really tired *. All the crowds had crunched their way home along the beach *.

So he said to his followers, 'Come with me across the lake'. They used the boat Jesus was already sit-ting in, and some other boats as well. They waded into the water *, pushed the boat further out * and clambered aboard *. They felt which way the wind was blowing by licking a finger and holding it up * and then hoisted the sail *.

Soon they were moving through the water, with the waves making a wash behind them *. Jesus lay down with his head on a pillow in the bottom of the boat and fell asleep *.

But then the wind started to whip up strongly * and that made the waves bigger and higher, crashing around the boat *. The water started to trickle in over the side of the boat * and they had to pull down the sail *. The disciples were getting frightened. 'Oh my goodness, this is terrible! Our boat is going to be completely swamped!' they shouted. They were scooping the water out as best they could, but the wind was still howling * and the sea was still churning and rolling all around and all over the boat *.

Then they noticed that Jesus was still fast asleep in the bottom of the boat! 'Wake up, Jesus', they said, shaking him, 'Do you care about us or not? We're going to drown soon if this weather goes on.'

Jesus woke up, looked at his friends, and saw the fear in their eyes. He heard the sounds of the angry wind * and the boiling, churning waves (*** above the next part of the story). He stood up in the boat and commanded the wind and waves to stop – he called out to them: 'Quiet! Be still!' * Then the wind stopped and the lake became calm, lapping gently around them again *.

Jesus looked round at his disciples. Their faces, hair and beards were soaked with sea spray, they were still panting from the effort of shouting and bailing out water, and they were standing ankle deep in water that had poured into the boat. They were completely stunned by what they had just seen. Who could this Jesus be if he could even take charge of the wind and waves? It was frightening to see such power in action.

Jesus said to them, 'Why are you afraid? Do you still have no faith?'

And they didn't really know what to say to him. One thing they had realised – that Jesus must be something more than an ordinary teacher – it was as if he had God's power.

They hoisted the sail again *, bailed out the rest of the water *, and sailed over the calm lake, with the water lapping the bow.

Praying

Use the prayer on the activity sheet.

Activities

Using the sheet they can make a model of the boat. Each child will need the right sized square of fabric (cut from an old sheet or shirt) so they can paint it and wrinkle it into waves. The boat is made from the cut-out drawings, with a used matchstick fixed in for the mast.

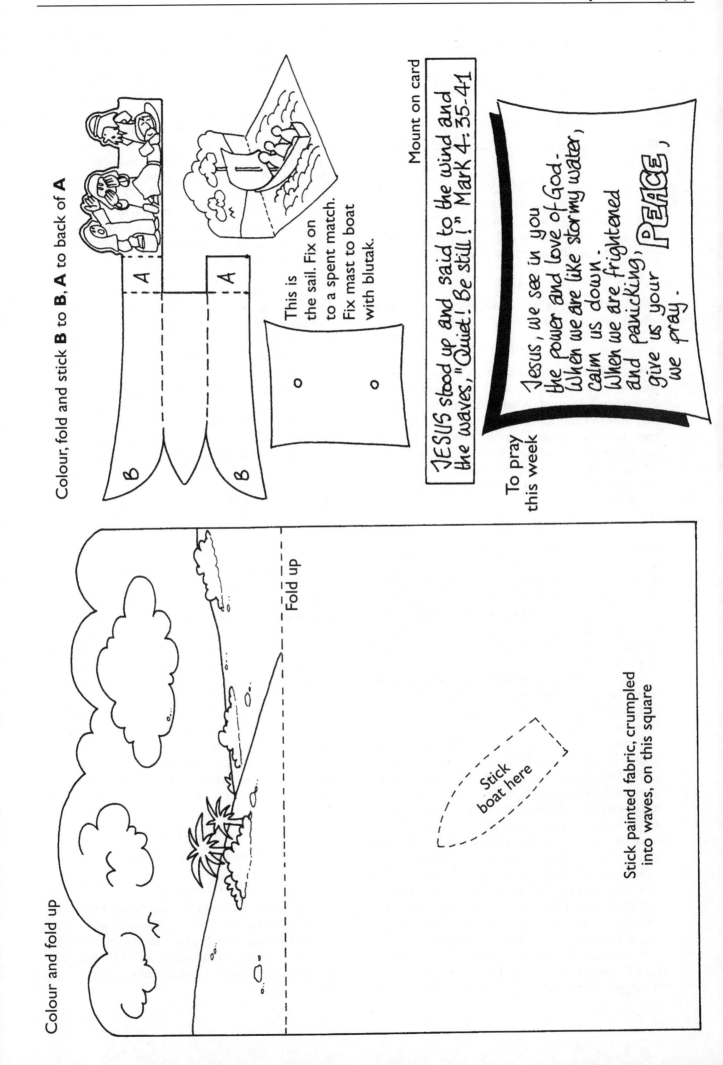

Colour, fold and stick **B** to **B**, **A** to back of **A**

A

A

B

B

This is the sail. Fix on to a spent match. Fix mast to boat with blutak.

Mount on card

JESUS stood up and said to the wind and the waves, "Quiet! Be still!" Mark 4.35-41

To pray this week

Jesus, we see in you the power and love of God. When we are like stormy water, calm us down. When we are frightened and panicking, give us your PEACE, we pray.

Colour and fold up

Fold up

Stick boat here

Stick painted fabric, crumpled into waves, on this square

PROPER 8

Thought for the day

God's power can reach even into death and draw out life.

Readings

2 Samuel 1:1, 17-27 or
Wisdom of Solomon 1:13-15; 2:23-24
Psalm 130 or Psalm 30 or Lamentations 3:23-33
2 Corinthians 8:7-15; Mark 5:21-43

Aim

To know the story of Jairus' daughter and the healing which 'interrupts' Jesus on his way to the house.

Starter

Provide all kinds of dressing-up clothes, including some thick gloves. Everyone sits in a circle, and a dice is passed round. When someone throws a six they run and start dressing up in all the clothes. If they manage to dress up in everything before another six is thrown, they can try peeling and eating a banana. As soon as someone else throws a six, they interrupt the first person and take the clothes for themselves.

Teaching

There's an interruption in our story today. Remind the children that Mark has written his Gospel to show us who Jesus is, and we've seen Jesus healing people, teaching people with his stories, and making the wind and waves do what he tells them. The disciples are beginning to realise that this is no ordinary teacher and healer – he seems to have the power of God in all he says and does.

Today we are going to travel with Jesus and his friends and see what happens. (Gather them all up and walk around, outside if possible, with you telling the story as you go.)

Explain that Jesus would often set off with his followers like this, walking from town to village to town. They would have passed by hills with sheep on them, fields growing barley and wheat, vineyards full of grapes, and farms with hens and their chicks. At the towns it became very crowded as the streets were narrow, and everyone came out to join them and see Jesus. Rumours about him being able to make people better meant that people would bring their sick friends and family out (stop walking), and Jesus would lay his hands on them and make them well again. Then everyone would be so happy, and join in the crowd! (Start walking again.)

Sometimes, instead of walking, Jesus and his friends would travel by boat across the lake. (Everyone climbs into a big 'fishing boat' and make the noises of the water. They look across at the shore – at the (pretend) crowd of people waiting for them. Everyone climbs out of the boat and stops.)

One man came up to Jesus and bowed. His name was Jairus, and he told Jesus that his twelve-year-old daughter was very ill, and asked Jesus to come and lay his hands on her so that she would be healed and live. So Jesus and his followers started to walk with Jairus to his house, down the narrow street. (Start walking.) But suddenly Jesus stopped walking and looked around. (Stop.) 'Who touched me?' he was asking. His friends said, 'Well, it's so crowded here that everyone is squashed against everyone else!' But Jesus had felt healing power go out of him and knew that someone had touched him wanting to be made better.

Then one of the women in the crowd came up to Jesus. 'It was me, teacher,' she said. 'I touched your clothes because I wanted to be made well – I've been ill for twelve years, you see. And thank you, Jesus, because you *have* made me better!'

So everyone went on walking to Jairus' house. (Start walking.) But then they were stopped again. (Stop.) Some men from the house came up to Jairus and whispered to him. Jairus burst into tears. (Can the children guess what the men had told him?) But Jesus paid no attention to what the men had said. He put his arm round Jairus. 'Don't be afraid,' he said. 'All you have to do is believe.'

Jesus told all the crowd to wait here, and only Peter, James and John, and Jairus and his wife were allowed to go on with him. (A leader takes three children and leaves the group to walk just out of sight.) So we'll stay here and wait for them to come back. (Sit down together, looking down towards the house. The healing party let out loud, excited shouts and come running back to the full group. Everyone gets up and crowds around them. The other leader continues the story. S/He excitedly explains how Jesus went into the house where the little girl was lying.) He held her hand, saying to her, 'Little girl, I tell you to stand up!' And sure enough she opened her eyes again and stood up, perfectly well, and Jesus had told her parents to give her something to eat!

(Walk with the group back to the usual meeting place, singing something like *Alleluia, alleluia, give thanks to the risen Lord* or *Oh! Oh! Oh! how good is the Lord.*)

Praying

Use the prayer on the activity sheet.

Activities

On the sheet there is a wordsearch to reinforce the teaching, and they can make a game to play which helps them imagine a typical day in Jesus' ministry. They will need some thin card on which to mount the game and pieces, once they have coloured them and cut them out.

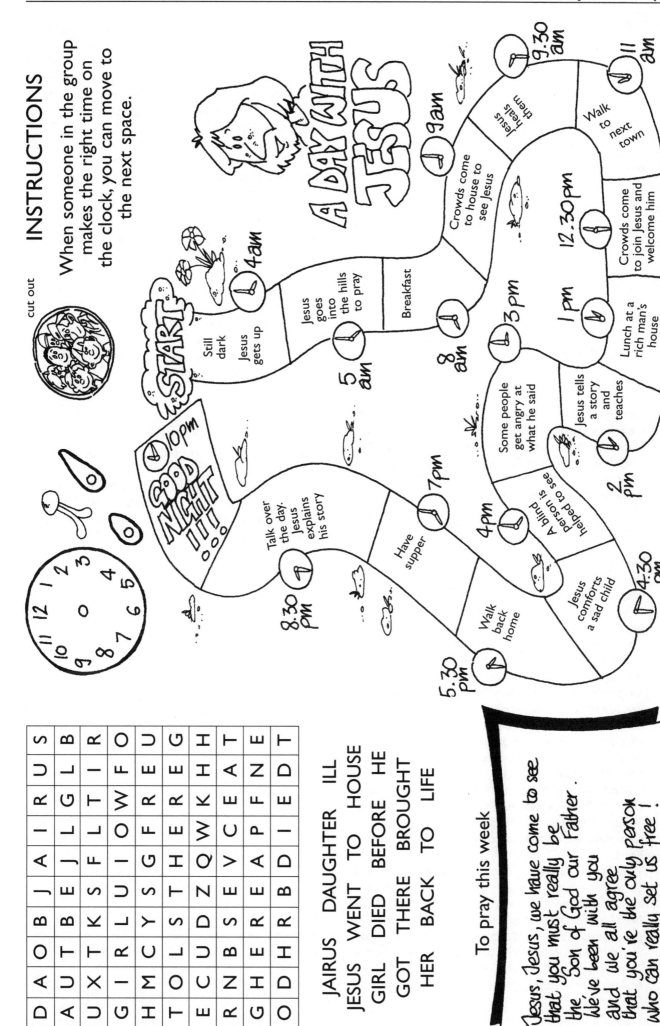

INSTRUCTIONS

When someone in the group makes the right time on the clock, you can move to the next space.

cut out

A DAY WITH JESUS

START

4am — Still dark Jesus gets up

5am — Jesus goes into the hills to pray

Breakfast

8am

9am — Crowds come to house to see Jesus

9.30 am — Jesus heals them

11 am — Walk to next town

12.30pm — Crowds come to join Jesus and welcome him

1pm — Lunch at a rich man's house

2pm — Jesus tells a story and teaches

3pm — Some people get angry at what he said

4pm — A blind person is helped to see

4.30 pm — Jesus comforts a sad child

5.30 pm — Walk back home

7pm — Have supper

8.30 pm — Talk over the day. Jesus explains his story

10pm — GOOD NIGHT!!!

Word Search

D	A	O	B	J	A	I	R	U	S
A	U	T	B	E	J	L	G	L	B
U	X	T	K	S	F	L	T	I	R
G	I	R	L	U	I	O	W	F	O
H	M	C	Y	S	G	F	R	E	U
T	O	L	S	T	H	E	R	E	G
E	C	U	D	Z	Q	W	K	H	H
R	N	B	S	E	V	C	E	A	T
G	H	E	R	E	A	P	F	N	E
O	D	H	R	B	D	I	E	D	T

JAIRUS   DAUGHTER   ILL
JESUS   WENT   TO   HOUSE
GIRL   DIED   BEFORE   HE
GOT   THERE   BROUGHT
HER   BACK   TO   LIFE

To pray this week

Jesus, Jesus, we have come to see
that you must really be
the Son of God our Father.
We've been with you
and we all agree
that you're the only person
who can really set us free!

PROPER 9

Sunday between 3 and 9 July inclusive

Thought for the day

If we are not ready to listen to the truth, we will not hear it.

Readings

2 Samuel 5:1-5, 9-10 or Ezekiel 2:1-5
Psalm 48 or Psalm 123
2 Corinthians 12:2-10
Mark 6:1-13

Aim

To learn about Jesus being listened to by some and not by others.

Starter

Sit in a circle so everyone is visible to everyone else. Choose someone present but don't let on who this is. Say, 'I'm thinking of someone who . . .', giving one clue at a time until the identity of the person has been guessed. The guesser carries on the game, until all the children who want to have had a go. With older children you could include some people who are in the church community.

Teaching

The people we have been describing are well known to us. Some of them we have known since they or we were babies. We perhaps go to the same school. That's how the people of Nazareth felt about Jesus – how could he be so special? To them he was just the ordinary Jesus they had always known, whose mother's name was Mary and whose father was the town's carpenter. They knew his brothers and sisters. They were happy for Jesus to make their furniture or repair their houses, but they didn't want to think of him as someone special who could teach them God's thoughts.

And because they didn't want to hear, they found they couldn't understand what Jesus was talking about. (We sometimes block our ears if there's something we don't want to hear.) Read the children Mark 6:1-6.

That was in Jesus' home town. What happened in all the other villages and towns? All the people crowded round to listen to him because when they heard him they felt close to God, and that felt really good. Jesus knew he'd never be able to get round everywhere for everyone to hear him so he had a plan. How many disciples were there? Twelve. (Lay down twelve simple paper cut-outs of people as

you say this.) Jesus split them into pairs (a child can do this), so how many pairs were there? Six.

He sent each pair of disciples out to the different villages and towns to preach to the people, encouraging them to change their hearts and their lives, to heal those who were ill and comfort those who were sad. (Spread the pairs out all over the floor.) And Jesus told them to go out just as they were, without money or luggage or insurance policies. They were to live simply and joyfully, and God would do the rest.

What do you think happened? There were still some who refused to listen, just as there are today. But lots and lots of people did listen to what they said, and turned back to God, and lots were healed.

Praying

Lord Jesus, help me to listen
with my heart as well as my ears.
Lord Jesus, speak into my thoughts and hopes,
my questions and my fears.
Amen.

Activities

On the sheet there are village doors to cut open. Like the pairs of disciples, they can knock at all the doors to tell the people of God's love for them, and some will open while others remain shut. They are also helped to remember the instructions Jesus gave to the disciples as they set out.

Notes

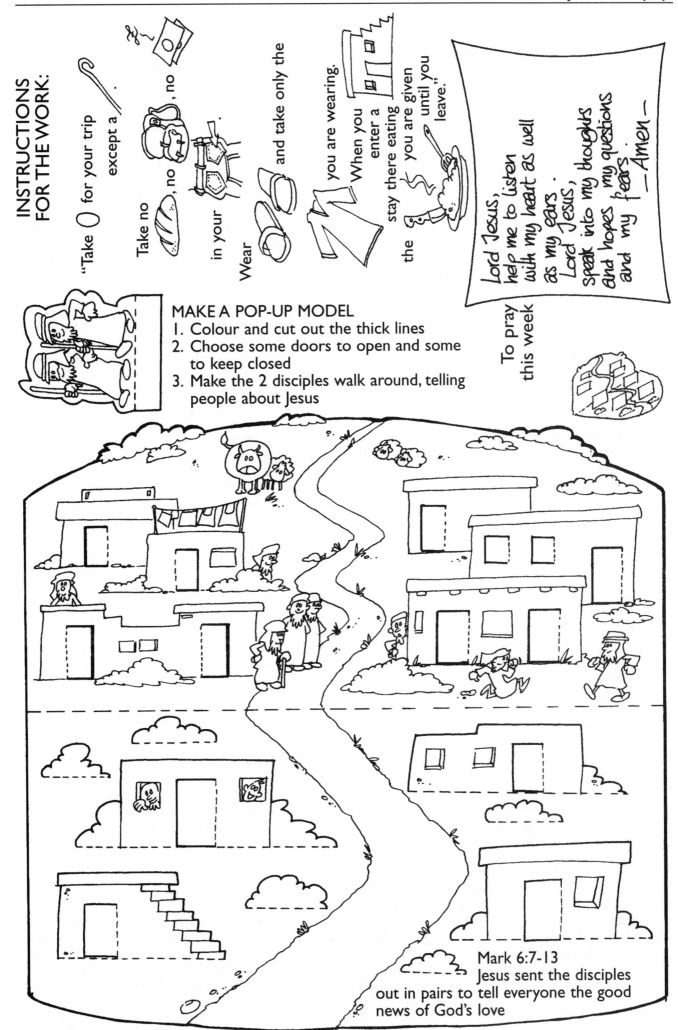

INSTRUCTIONS FOR THE WORK:

"Take ◯ for your trip except a ⌒ .

Take no ◯, no ◯, no ◯ in your ◯

Wear ◯ and take only the ◯ you are wearing.

When you enter a ◯ stay there eating the ◯ you are given until you leave."

Lord Jesus,
help me to listen
with my heart as well
as my ears .
Lord Jesus,
speak into my thoughts
and hopes, my questions
and my fears. —Amen—

To pray this week

MAKE A POP-UP MODEL
1. Colour and cut out the thick lines
2. Choose some doors to open and some to keep closed
3. Make the 2 disciples walk around, telling people about Jesus

Mark 6:7-13
Jesus sent the disciples out in pairs to tell everyone the good news of God's love

PROPER 10

Sunday between 10 and 16 July inclusive

Thought for the day

Those who speak out God's will are bound to be vulnerable to rejection and abuse.

Readings

2 Samuel 6:1-5, 12b-19 or Amos 7:7-15
Psalm 24 or Psalm 85:8-13
Ephesians 1:3-14
Mark 6:14-29

Aim

To know the events surrounding the death of John the Baptist.

Starter

'Please can I have . . .' Ask for various things which the group have to work together to bring you. Here are some ideas of what to ask for: a piece of paper with three signatures on it; eight feet in a row; Mark 6:24; a human chain; a round of applause.

Teaching

Use last week's paper disciples, scattered in pairs and busy telling everyone how they can be put right with God and live in the light of God's love.

Meanwhile, back at Herod's palace (place down a cut-out crown), King Herod's conscience is giving him a bad time. He hears about all the signs and miracles and thinks Jesus must be John the Baptist come back to life. Why does he think that? Because it was Herod who had ordered John the Baptist to be killed, and he still badly regretted it. Today we're going to find out how it was that John the Baptist's head ended up on a plate at one of Herod's birthday parties. (Place a silver serving dish down.) It's a gruesome tale.

(As you tell the story use the following props: chess pieces for the king and queen, a silk scarf and pair of dancing shoes, and a jagged cut-out shape of bright red with the word 'Hate' written on it, and a cup cake with a birthday candle on it.)

King Herod had got himself a new wife, whose name was Queen Herodias. (Place chess pieces side by side.) The trouble was Herodias had been the wife of Herod's brother and it wasn't right for Herod to marry her. John the Baptist bravely told Herod that it wasn't right for him to be married to his brother's wife. So, as you can imagine, Queen Herodias hated John the Baptist with a great big

hate! (Place the 'Hate' sign down, just above the Queen.) She wanted very badly to have John killed, but she couldn't do that because she knew her new husband liked listening to John and respected him, even if he didn't always like what John said.

Then came the perfect time for Queen Herodias to get her way. It was Herod's birthday (place down the birthday cake) and there was to be a big party with lots of important people there. Herodias had a daughter who came to the party, and after the meal she danced for King Herod and his guests. (Place down the silky scarf and shoes, and everyone can sing some slinky dance music.) When she had finished dancing, everyone clapped. (Everyone claps.) Herod was so pleased with her dancing that he did a rather foolish thing. He told her she could have anything she asked for – even half his kingdom! And all the important guests heard him say it.

She went to Herodias, her mother, and said, 'What should I ask the king to give me?'

Can you guess what Herodias answered? She said to her daughter, 'Ask for the head of John the Baptist on a serving plate.' John was in prison at the time. So the girl went quickly back to the king and asked for the head of John the Baptist – on a serving plate.

King Herod was really sad. The last thing he wanted to do was have John killed, but he had just told the princess she could have anything she asked for, and he didn't want to look silly or weak in front of all those important guests he had invited to his birthday party. So he gave the order, and John was beheaded in prison. They put his head on a serving plate and brought it in to the party. King Herod gave it to the princess, and she gave it to her mother. John, who had helped so many people get to know the love of God, was killed because he had spoken out God's truth, and Herodias hated him for it.

Talk with the children about what they think Herod should have done at his birthday party, recognising the pressures we all have to take the easier choice instead of sticking to what we know is right.

Praying

Father, we thank you for the courage
of people like John the Baptist,
speaking out your truth
even when it put their lives in danger.
Give us the courage to live your way
and speak out your truth,
as we work with you
for the coming of the kingdom.

Activities

On the sheet there are stories of Christians who have been imprisoned or persecuted for their faith, and still consider it to have been the right thing to do. They will also be making a talking face to remind them to natter and chatter the good news.

How to make your hand into a talking face!

1. Tuck your thumb inside your fist
2. Draw on eyes, nose and mouth
3. Wiggle your thumb and watch your hand talking!

Peter was thrown into prison for telling people about Jesus.
Was it worth it, Peter?

YES!

Dietrich Bonhoeffer was imprisoned for fighting against evil ideas.
Would you do the same again, Dietrich?

YES!

Sheila Cassidy was put in prison for treating a patient the government didn't like. Would you do the same thing again, Sheila?

YES!

'WHOEVER GIVES UP HIS LIFE FOR ME AND FOR THE GOOD NEWS WILL HAVE TRUE LIFE FOR EVER.' (Mark 8:35)

O									
W	H	O	E	V	E	R	A	J	P
K	G	I	N	E	O	T	H	E	U
F	O	R	S	F	N	O	R	M	E
I	A	N	D	I	B	E	Y	U	W
G	O	O	D	L	H	R	W	Q	E
I	D	M	S	A	L	C	I	S	V
V	H	A	V	E	R	B	L	Z	E
E	F	T	C	P	O	V	L	D	R
S	U	E	L	I	F	E	B	X	A

To pray this week

Father, we thank you for the courage
of people like John the Baptist,
speaking out your truth even
when it put their lives in danger.
Give us the courage to live your way
and speak out your truth,
as we work with you
for the coming of the kingdom.

PROPER 11

Sunday between 17 and 23 July inclusive

Thought for the day

Like a good shepherd, Jesus sees the needs of his people and always responds with love.

Readings

2 Samuel 7:1-14a or Jeremiah 23:1-6
Psalm 89:20-37 or Psalm 23
Ephesians 2:11-22
Mark 6:30-34, 53-56

Aim

To know what a typical day in Jesus' ministry would have been like.

Starter

Have a clock face and arrange with the children that when it says 7 o'clock it's time to get up, 9 o'clock it's working time at school, 12 o'clock it's lunchtime, 4 o'clock is watching television, and at midnight everyone is fast asleep. When the clock time is displayed and called out, they do the appropriate actions.

Teaching

Beforehand prepare a blue sheet to look like a motorway sign for services, based on the picture below.

You will also need a 30 mph sign and a sign for a carpenter's shop, together with a few wood-working tools and bits of wood, and a pair of sandals.

Begin by sharing a couple of different typical days from the group, one child and one adult, starting at waking-up time and going through to bedtime. Today we are going to take a look at a typical day in the life of Jesus during the years of his ministry.

Jesus grew up helping Joseph in the carpentry business the family owned. (Place down the carpenter's sign, the wood and the tools.) When he was grown-up he carried on working as a carpenter, sawing wood, hammering in nails, measuring, sanding down and polishing. During this time he lived at home, probably eating with the rest of his family in the evening after work.

When he reached the age of thirty (place down the 30 mph sign) things changed. Jesus stopped being a carpenter (pack the tools and wood away) and started the work God needed him to do among the people. Instead of living at home and being sure of a bed to sleep on and food to eat, Jesus set out walking around the country (place down the sandals), staying with friends, or sleeping rough.

(Now refer to the service station sign.) Jesus ate and drank wherever he and his disciples were invited, and whatever they were given. Sometimes this would be grand parties at the houses of rich, important people, sometimes they might be crowded into poor people's homes, laughing and talking late into the night, and sometimes they might go hungry. Sometimes they would stay for a few days or a few weeks with people, and sometimes there wouldn't be any shelter provided. Jesus once said, 'Foxes have holes and the birds have their nests but the Son of Man has nowhere to lay his head.' They never knew for certain in the morning where they might be that evening as Jesus just went where he sensed God wanted him to go. For transport they used feet, walking along the roads and tracks between the towns and villages.

So what was the work Jesus was doing for these two or three years? There were people who needed healing and comforting, forgiving and setting free from evil spirits. There were people living in the darkness of evil who needed to have God's light brought into their lives. There was lots to tell people about God so they understood how lovely he was, and there was the work of helping people learn to love one another and help one another. All of this was like the job of a shepherd – caring for the people and guiding them wisely.

And if we had lived in one of the towns or villages around the lake of Galilee at that time – nearly two thousand years ago, we'd have met Jesus; perhaps he would have eaten with us, or stayed at our house, or healed one of our friends, or played with us.

Praying

Be with us in the morning –
from the first yawn to the coco pops.
Be with us in school –
from 2+2 till the last full stop.
Be with us in the evening –
from the children's programmes till bedtime.
Be with us while we sleep –
from starlight to the new day's dawn.
Amen.

Activities

The children can make a day-round prayer with their usual day on one side, and a day in Jesus' ministry on the other. They will each need a paper fastener, and some thin card for strengthening the circles.

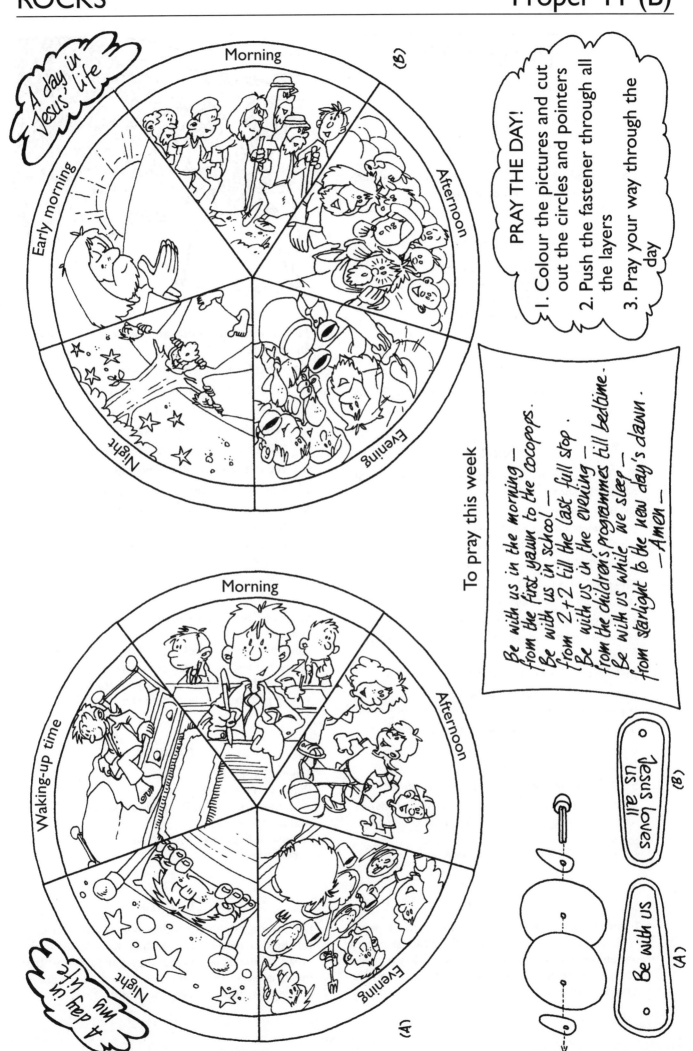

A day in Jesus' life

PRAY THE DAY!
1. Colour the pictures and cut out the circles and pointers
2. Push the fastener through all the layers
3. Pray your way through the day

To pray this week

Be with us in the morning —
from the first yawn to the cocopps.
Be with us in school —
from 2+2 till the last full stop.
Be with us in the evening —
from the children's programmes till bedtime.
Be with us while we sleep —
from starlight to the new day's dawn.
— Amen —

Jesus loves us all (B)

Be with us (A)

A day in my life

Proper 12

Sunday between 24 and 30 July inclusive

Thought for the day

Out of God's riches, a great crowd is fed and satisfied from a small offering of food.

Readings

2 Samuel 11:1-15 or 2 Kings 4:42-44
Psalm 14 or Psalm 145:10-18
Ephesians 3:14-21
John 6:1-21

Aim

To look at the meaning of the feeding of the five thousand.

Starter

Teach the children the song *5000+ hungry folk* with actions as shown below.

5 0 0 0+ hungry folk,
(five fingers on one hand, make ring with other hand which is shown three times, then rub tummies)

came 4 2 listen 2 Jesus. *(cup hand to ear)*

The 6 x 2 said O O O,
(use fingers for each number and for the O)

where can we get some food from?
(shrug shoulders and open hands, moving head from side to side)

Just 1 had 1 2 3 4 5, *(use fingers)*

loaves and 1 2 fishes. *(count with fingers)*

When Jesus blessed the 5 + 2
(hands face down as if blessing; count with fingers)

they were increased many x over.
(roly-poly with hands going upwards)

5 0 0 0+ 8 it up, *(use fingers, then pretend to eat)*

with 1 2 3 4 5 6 7 8 9 10 11 12 basketfuls left over.
(count on fingers and stamp each foot for 11 and 12)

(Ian Smale
© Copyright 1985 Kingsway's Thankyou Music)

Here are the questions and references for finding the answers:

1. What lake did Jesus sail over? John 6:1
2. What time of year was it? John 6:4
3. What did Jesus say to Philip? John 6:5
4. What did Philip reply? John 6:7
5. What food did the boy offer? John 6:9
6. What did Jesus tell the people to do? John 6:10
7. How many people were there? John 6:10
8. What two things did Jesus do with the food? John 6:11
9. What happened to the food left over? John 6:12-13
10. What did this miracle make the people want to do? John 6:15

Give out Bibles and help everyone to find John chapter 6. Then as each question is asked, the children can tell the story, checking with the Bible as they go. As each question is answered, take it off the picture and lay it at the side, until you are left with the whole picture and the whole story revealed.

Praying

Loving Father,
thank you for feeding us
with food for our bodies and our souls,
making us strong
so we can live good, loving lives.
Amen.

Teaching

Beforehand prepare some pieces of card or paper with questions on one side and the bible references on the other. Arrange them question side up over a picture of the feeding of the crowd, based on the drawing below.

Activities

On the sheet there is a coded message to crack, and the link is made with another time Jesus broke bread at the Passover, so they can see how that bread goes on being broken to feed Christians in every generation all over the world.

And the feeding goes on, and on, and on, and on …

Q: Why did Jesus escape into the hills?

A: Because he knew that

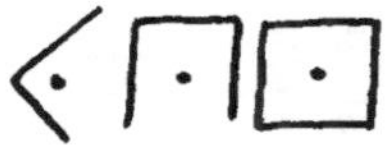

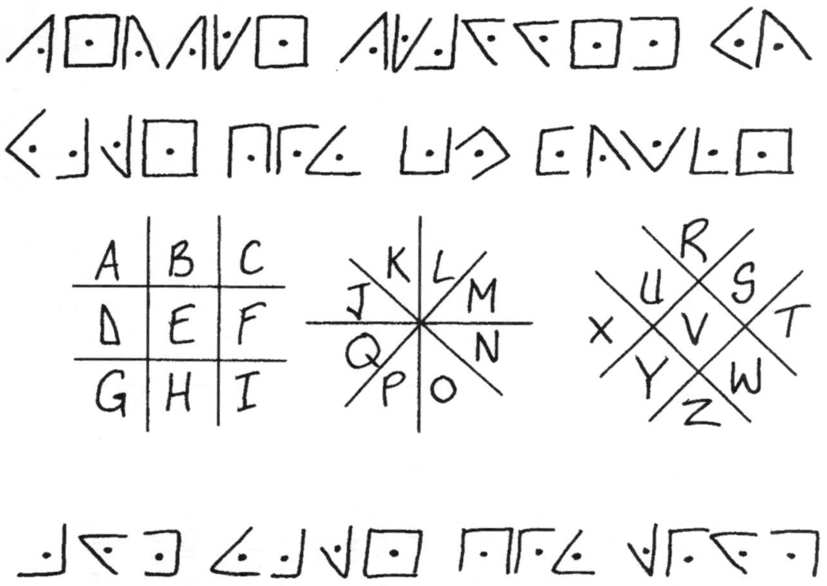

(puzzle — pigpen cipher)

A	B	C
D	E	F
G	H	I

J	K	L	M
	N		
	Q	P	O

(pigpen cipher grids with R S T / U V / X Y W Z)

(John 6, verse 15)

To pray this week

Loving Father,
thank you for feeding us
with food for our
bodies and our souls,
making us strong
so we can live
good, loving lives. Amen-

PROPER 13

Thought for the day

Jesus is the Bread of Life who satisfies our hunger and sustains us on our journey to heaven.

Readings

2 Samuel 11:26-12:13a or Exodus 16:2-4, 9-15
Psalm 51:1-12 or Psalm 78:23-29
Ephesians 4:1-16
John 6:24-35

Aim

To look at what it means for Jesus to be the Bread of Life.

Starter

Beforehand draw pictures of several different meals (or cut pictures from magazines). Cut these into wedge-shaped servings and scatter them all around the room. The children find the separate pieces and put them together so they end up with complete meals.

Teaching

Look at the different kinds of meals we have made, and at the variety we like to eat during the week and during each day. If we put all the things we ate in a week together, it would be quite a lot, and even though we feel nice and satisfied just after we've eaten breakfast, we're still looking forward to lunch by the end of the morning and tea by the evening.

God has provided us with a rich planet to live on which has plenty of food for us to eat – there's enough for everyone if only we were better at sharing. We use the fruits, roots and vegetables that grow in it, and the animals, birds and fish that live there. God has provided wonderfully for our bodies.

Remind the children of last week when Jesus fed that huge crowd of five thousand people with bread and fish. That was a different kind of feeding in a way, because Jesus was looking after them spiritually as well as physically. The next day after that the people went out searching for Jesus again. They had been very impressed by all that bread and fish and they were hoping for some more.

But Jesus said, 'Don't just run after the kind of food that satisfies the body. The body won't last for ever – some time it will die. A much better idea is to run after the kind of bread which will feed you spiritually, so that you'll stay spiritually alive and healthy, even after you're dead.'

So the people thought that sounded the best kind of bread, but they didn't know how to get hold of it. They'd never seen any in the baker's. They said to Jesus, 'Give us this kind of bread, sir. We'd like to live on that bread which gives life which lasts for ever.'

Then Jesus looked round at them and said, 'My Father has given you the true bread from heaven to give life to the world, and it's standing right here in front of you. It's me! I am the bread that gives you life!'

Jesus meant that just as ordinary bread is very good at satisfying us and keeping us physically alive and healthy, so Jesus himself is the one we need to believe in and be with for spiritual life which goes on whether we're still alive here or whether our bodies have worn out and died. In Jesus we can go on being very much alive for ever, just as Jesus is.

Praying

Jesus, I know that you were born as a baby,
lived and worked among us,
showing us God's love,
that you died on the cross and rose again to life.
I know you are alive for ever
and I want to stay close to you
right through this life
and on into heaven. Amen.

Activities

On the sheet there are different ways of 'feeding on Jesus, the Bread of Life' which the children can do. Help them to get around their Bibles so they know exactly where to find the Gospels – there are references of familiar events for them to practise looking them up. Some of the children will already be receiving communion at church; for others this is something for the future.

Notes

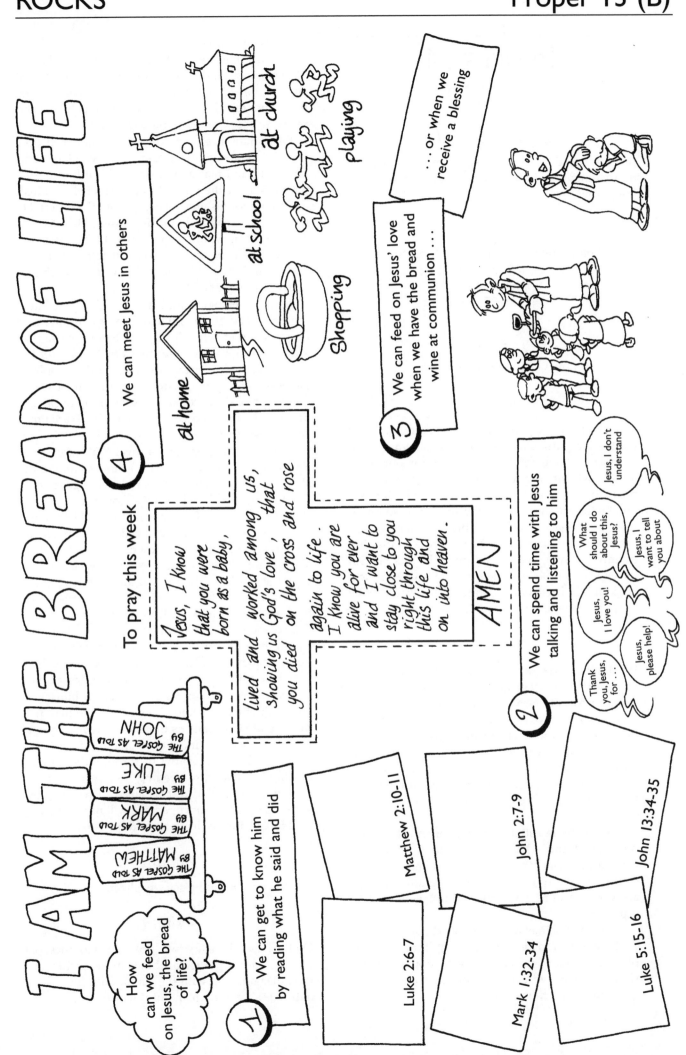

PROPER 14

Sunday between 7 and 13 August inclusive

Thought for the day

Just as bread is the visible form of life-giving nourishment, so Jesus is the visible form of God's life-giving love.

Readings

2 Samuel 18:5-9, 15, 31-33 or 1 Kings 19:4-8
Psalm 130 or Psalm 34:1-8
Ephesians 4:25-5:2
John 6:35, 41-51

Aim

To look at how God leads and feeds us.

Starter

Have a variety of ordinary objects laid out. As you tell them a particular use, they choose which item is most suitable for the job. Ideas for objects: a toothbrush, an umbrella, an egg cup, a loaf of bread, a crayon and a washing-up bowl. The uses will be the obvious ones, but also include some for which no object is available, but for which one of the objects might possibly be pressed into use. For example, 'having a drink in' might be linked with the egg cup or the washing up-bowl, and 'writing a book' might use a crayon, though this wouldn't be terribly efficient.

Teaching

We don't always want the jobs we're given in life, because they're not always easy. Mostly, jobs we are given turn out to be a mixture of bits we enjoy very much and bits we'd rather not be doing, because they are difficult. A clown may enjoy doing silly things to make everyone laugh, but not enjoy getting all his make-up off before he goes to bed. A drummer in a group may love practising and performing, but hate having to get up really early to travel on to the next concert.

One of the questions humans often ask is this: 'Who am I and what am I here for?' (Have this written out clearly.) If toothbrushes and egg cups could ask that question it would be quite easy to answer – 'You're a toothbrush and you exist to brush teeth.'

As human beings we need to work together with God our Maker to answer that question, as God has plans for each of us, and work he hopes we will want to share with him during the time we are given to live on this earth.

Today we are going to look at one of God's friends from the Old Testament who wasn't finding life very easy, and was wondering what it was all about. (Spread out a large sheet or towel on the floor and tell the story with the help of cut-out pictures, based on those on page 133.)

Elijah had been working hard telling people about God, and showing them how wonderful and power-ful and real he is. That had got him on the wrong side of the wicked queen Jezebel, so Elijah had to run for his life and escape into the desert. He felt lonely, exhausted and depressed. He was also starving hungry and very thirsty. Elijah sat down under a bush and wanted to die, he felt so bad. 'I've had enough, Lord,' he prayed. 'Let me die. I'm no better than my ancestors!'

God felt very sorry for his friend Elijah. He knew the job he had given him to do was a hard one, and he understood why Elijah was feeling so fed-up with it all. But God knew that Elijah was still the one he wanted to speak his word to the people of Israel – what Elijah needed at the moment was a good night's sleep, some rest, something to eat and drink and a bit of peace and quiet. (There are times we all need that.)

So first of all God gave a lovely gift of sleep to Elijah. He slept and slept for hours, under the shade of a tree. Then God sent a messenger to give Elijah some food. When Elijah opened his eyes, there was a warm, freshly baked loaf of bread and a jar of clear water. That cheered Elijah up. He ate and drank and then lay down and went back to sleep again. He was *so* tired! When he woke up next time the Lord told him to eat and drink again, so that he'd have the energy for the journey God wanted him to make. Elijah sat up and ate and drank, and started to feel better. He knew God was calling him to walk to the holy mountain, and he knew that he could trust God to look after him, even through the very worst and most tiring times.

Many centuries later, Jesus talked of himself as being 'the Bread of Life'. Like Elijah, we may find that the life God calls us to is not always easy, and we will sometimes find it tiring and hard work. But God will always look after us through those times, leading us and also feeding us with whatever strength, energy and rest we need. If we keep our spiritual eyes and ears open, we will notice the way God looks after us, leads us and feeds us.

Praying

Use the prayer on the activity sheet.

Activities

On the sheet there are two 'noticing' activities, one looking out for particular things in the picture and the other noticing with the eye of faith how God's nature is shown in the natural world.

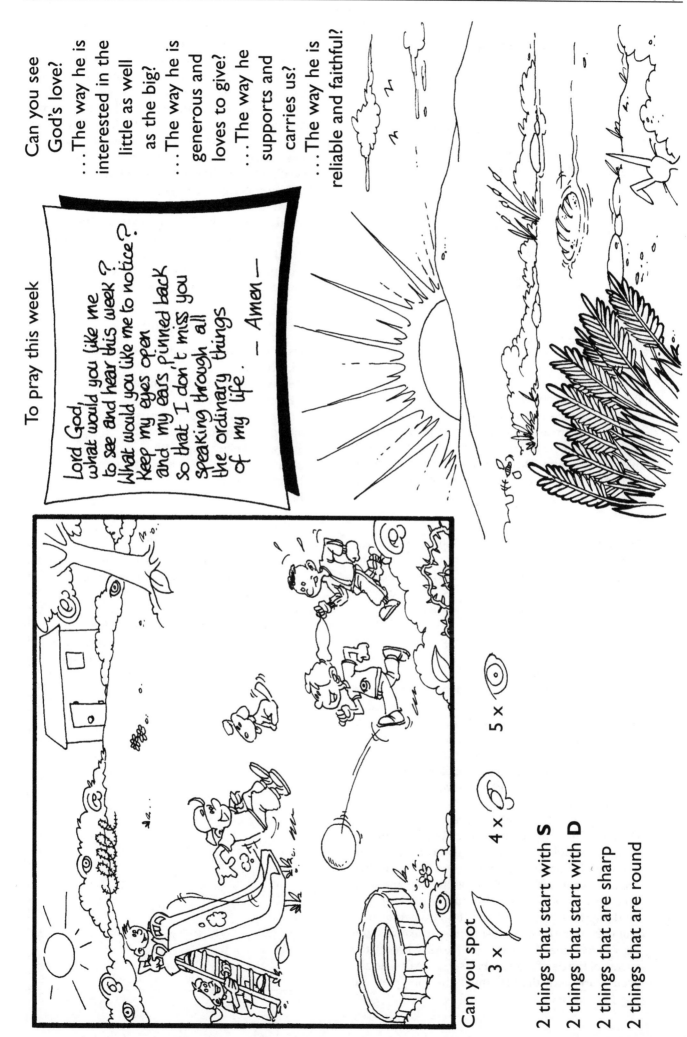

Can you see God's love?
...The way he is interested in the little as well as the big?
...The way he is generous and loves to give?
...The way he supports and carries us?
...The way he is reliable and faithful?

To pray this week

Lord God,
what would you like me
to see and hear this week?
What would you like me to notice?
Keep my eyes open
and my ears pinned back
so that I don't miss you
speaking through all
the ordinary things
of my life. — Amen —

Can you spot

3 x

4 x

5 x

2 things that start with **S**

2 things that start with **D**

2 things that are sharp

2 things that are round

PROPER 15

Sunday between 14 and 20 August inclusive

Thought for the day

God's wisdom may appear foolishness without the God-given grace to understand.

Readings

1 Kings 2:10-12; 3:3-14 or Proverbs 9:1-6
Psalm 111 or Psalm 34:9-14
Ephesians 5:15-20
John 6:51-58

Aim

To know that God is wise.

Starter

Tell or read a story which illustrates wisdom, such as the Emperor's new clothes, or the crowded house story, where a man complaining of his pokey home is advised by a wise man to get all kinds of animals to live in it with him. Then he is told to let them all go, and he ends up discovering how much space he has.

Teaching

The child who spoke out and said the Emperor was really wearing no clothes at all was wise because he stuck with what he knew was real and true. The man who advised the farmer to fill his home up with animals and then have it to himself again was wise because he knew about people. He knew that we grumble when we want something we can't have, and that we're happy if what we have is better than what we used to have.

So we can be wise even if we don't get top marks for our spellings every week. We can be wise whether we are grown-up or still children. And sometimes children are a lot better at being wise than grown-ups! In fact, some of the wisest grown-ups are the ones who still go on thinking like children, still asking questions and marvelling at the world, still saying what they know is true.

As you can imagine, our great God is full of wisdom. That doesn't mean that he knows everything (although he does), but it means that God really understands why people act the way they do, and what makes each of us like we are. And because God is wise, he also knows the best way for things to happen. If we pray every day for God's will to be done on earth just as it is in heaven, then we can be sure that God will work with all the events of the day for good. He is so wise that he can even work with the bad things that happen, the

arguments and fights, the disappointments and wrong choices people make.

(Place a large question mark on the floor.) If we are not at all sure how to put things right when we've made mistakes (place a cross over the question mark), our wise God can help us. (Place the question mark down again.) If we are bothered by things that are happening at school or at our club or at home (place the cross over the question mark), our wise God knows how to work in that place so that things are sorted out for good.

As God's children we are to live wisely as well. How do we do that? We need to go through life looking and listening. We need to seek God out every day. And we need to make good use of every opportunity we have for playing on God's team, fighting evil and working for good.

Praying

Jesus, did I hear you needed players on your team?
Well, here I am!
Did I hear you needed volunteers?
That's me!
I want to be on your side, Jesus,
fighting for good against evil,
fighting for justice and truth
with weapons of love and hope.
Who's for Jesus?
ME!

Activities

On the sheet there is a picture in which to spot the opportunities for doing good. These are not all immediately obvious, just as real opportunities are often hard to spot. Help the children to see the situations where conditions might be improved, people in difficulty helped, and others comforted or befriended. There is also a kind of crossword puzzle containing practical advice for anyone wanting to be wise.

Notes

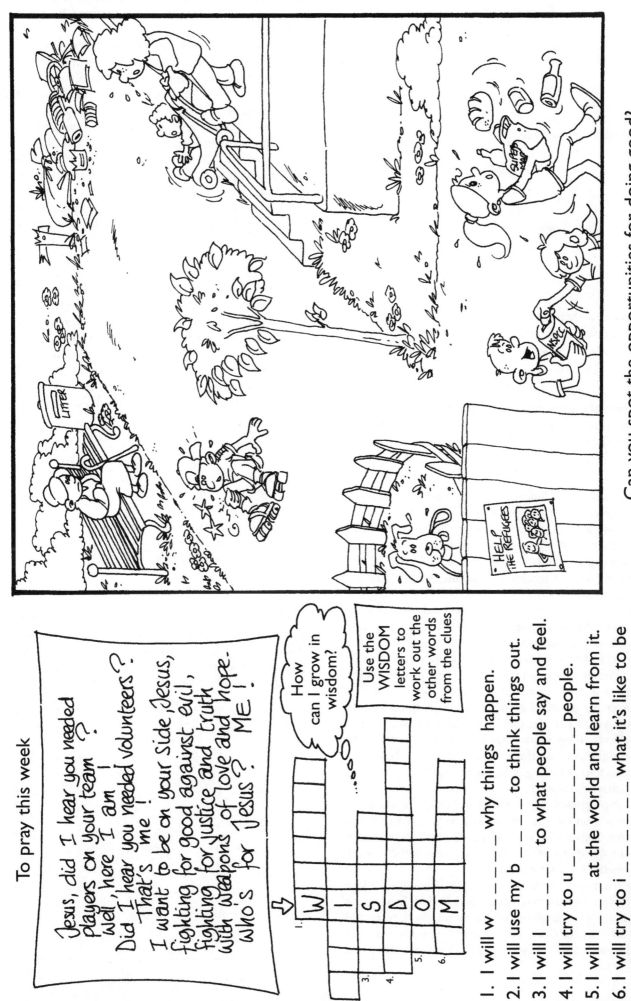

Can you spot the opportunities for doing good?

To pray this week

Jesus, did I hear you needed
players on your team?
Well, here I am!
Did I hear you needed volunteers?
That's me!
I want to be on your side, Jesus,
fighting for good against evil,
fighting for justice and truth
with weapons of love and hope.
Who's for Jesus? Me!

How can I grow in wisdom?

Use the WISDOM letters to work out the other words from the clues

1. I will w _ _ _ _ _ why things happen.
2. I will use my b _ _ _ _ to think things out.
3. I will l _ _ _ _ _ to what people say and feel.
4. I will try to u _ _ _ _ _ _ _ _ _ people.
5. I will l _ _ _ at the world and learn from it.
6. I will try to i _ _ _ _ _ _ what it's like to be other people

AND THEN YOU'LL GROW TO BE WISE!

PROPER 16

Sunday between 21 and 27 August inclusive

Thought for the day

'To whom else could we go? You alone have the words of eternal life.'

Readings

1 Kings 8:(1, 6, 10-11) 22-30, 41-43 or
Joshua 24:1-2a, 14-18
Psalm 84 or Psalm 34:15-22
Ephesians 6:10-20
John 6:56-69

Aim

To know that some of Jesus' followers turned away and only those who recognised him as the Holy One of God stayed with him.

Starter

Play 'follow my leader' with different children taking the lead in dancing to some music. They all do what the leader does.

Teaching

Lay out the following items to serve as memory joggers: a packet of mustard seed (or any small seeds), a coin and a toy sheep. Remind everyone that while Jesus was travelling around the country-side during the two or three years of his ministry, he did lots of teaching by telling stories. Use the objects for them to recall the kingdom growing like a tiny seed grows into a big tree, God searching for sinners like a woman searches for one lost coin and a shepherd for one lost sheep. The people were used to hearing Jesus explaining things like this.

Perhaps they can remember Mum or Dad telling them it must be about bedtime. They know that probably means that they needn't jump up and go just yet. But if the tone of voice changes and gets serious, they know that means they have to go straightaway, as this time it's for real! They have been told not in a gentle, roundabout way, but very clearly and directly.

Now place down a loaf of bread. When Jesus started telling the people that he was living bread from heaven, he was talking to them very clearly and directly. He was showing them that he really was the Holy One of God.

That left them with quite a challenge. (Place down two separate cards, one labelled 'Jesus must be a liar!' and the other 'Jesus must really be the Holy One of God'. Place a question mark between the two cards. They could see that they either had

to believe him, and recognise him as the Christ, or not believe him, in which case he must be a liar who had let them down.

How would they choose? (Place down a picture of an eye.) They could think over all the things they had seen Jesus do. Did they point to him being a liar or the Christ? (Place down a picture of an ear.) They could think over all the teaching they had heard, and the way he had talked to people. Did his words point to him being a liar or the Christ? (Place down a scroll.) They could think over what their prophets had said about the Christ. Did Jesus fit in with those ideas or not?

We are told that for many of those people the thought of this Jesus they knew being the Christ was just too difficult to accept, and they turned away and walked off. For other people, although it seemed incredible that the Christ was actually standing on the grass beside them, they realised that everything pointed to Jesus telling the truth, so he must really be the Holy One of God. And that made them very happy and excited indeed!

When Jesus saw some of the crowd moving away, he turned and looked at his disciples and asked them if they would be going as well. Let's find out what they said. (Look up John 6:67-69 and read it out.)

Praying

Jesus, Jesus, we have come to see
that you must really be
the Son of God our Father.
We've been with you and we all agree
that only in your service
can the world be truly free!

Activities

On the sheet there is a puzzle to work out so that they come to discover Peter's words – 'You are the Holy One of God'. They are also encouraged to think through the reasons for claiming that Jesus was declaring the truth about himself.

Notes

98

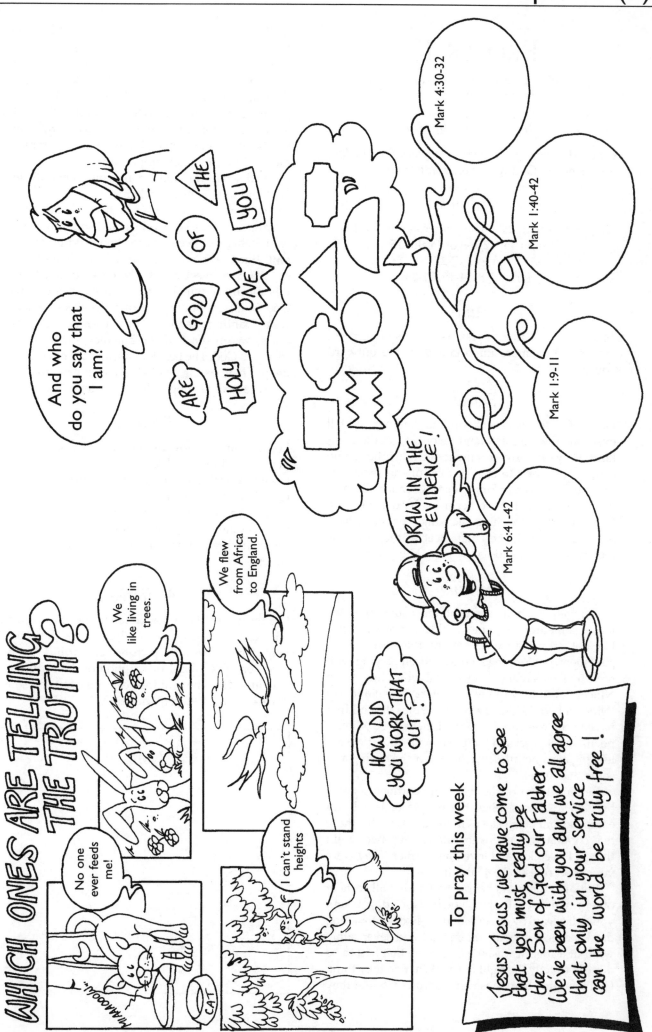

PROPER 17

Sunday between 28 August and 3 September inclusive

Thought for the day

We need to be careful never to replace the timeless commands of God with man-made traditions.

Readings

Song of Solomon 2:8-13 or Deuteronomy 4:1-2, 6-9
Psalm 45:1-2, 6-9 or Psalm 15
James 1:17-27
Mark 7:1-8, 14-15, 21-23

Aim

To understand that, as far as God is concerned, the 'inside' is more important than the outward appearance.

Starter

Fix down a few sheets of paper to the floor and tell everyone they are in a land belonging to the great king. They can move around to the music but on no account are they to step on one of the sheets, as these belong to the king's enemy. Gradually add more sheets so that it becomes harder to walk freely. Anyone touching the king's enemy's land has to stay banished on that sheet, as they are now too 'unclean' to tread on the great king's land.

Teaching

Talk together about some of the ritual rules we make, sometimes as games and sometimes for real, like not letting ourselves step on the cracks in the pavement, or stopping all the children playing with their toys by saying some special word, like 'Poop Nincom' (but they can when you reverse it and say 'Nincom Poop'!). Share any ritual rules the children have used. You could also read them A. A. Milne's poem about cracks in the pavement. Today we are looking at some rules which are worth keeping and some that aren't.

Remind them of the ten commandments given by God to Moses when the people of Israel had escaped from being slaves in Egypt. Basically, these ten commandments were all saying two main things: Love God and love one another. They were very good rules to keep and live by.

But over the years people had added all sorts of other ritual rules. To show you loved God, you kept yourself 'clean' by all sorts of rules like not touching dead bodies, not eating certain food, and never eating without a special washing ceremony that had to be done in exactly the right order. (What do they think God thought about those kind of rules? Would they really show that the people loved him? Or would they just show that the people had a lot of rules?)

Read from Mark 7, verses 1, 2 and 5. So Jesus, the Son of God, wasn't keeping all the little tiny rules as the religious leaders thought he ought to. When they picked him up on it, Jesus told them this: 'You think it's more important to follow your own rules than God's commandments! But it's God's commandments which are really important.'

(And what are God's commandments? To love God and to love one another.)

That's just as true for us as it was for them. We may have got ourselves clean and smart to come to church, because we want to show God he's important. But God's more interested in whether we've got ready to meet him by being kind and helpful this morning, whether we've been in touch with God at all by praying during the week, whether we're wanting to show off or not. Those things may not show on the outside, but they show up very clearly to God. The best-looking and the best-dressed people here as far as God is concerned, are those who are really trying to live the way of love.

Praying

Lord, I want to show my love and thanks
in the way I live my life.
I want everything I think, say and do
to be in line with your Law of love.
Lord, help me to be more concerned
with the state of my soul before you
than with my efforts to impress other people.
Amen.

Activities

On the sheet there are different people needing advice, and the group can think of how they could help. There are also pictures of various people together with a brief description of their attitudes and lifestyle. The children can look out for some marks of 'true religion' in them

---

Notes

Pam is rich and bored. She needs some advice for something worthwhile to do with her time and money.

Joyce is sour and crabby because she hasn't ever forgiven her son for leaving home.

Mick is fed up because he's in prison again for stealing.

Cathy has suddenly remembered that Mum told her to be home by 4 o'clock.

Nick has just found a diamond ring. What should he do?

GOOD ADVICE NEEDED!

HELP! HELP!

Can you give some good advice to them all

HINT Base your advice on this

LOVE GOD; LOVE ONE ANOTHER

SPOT THE TRUE RELIGION

Julie goes to church every week. She goes and spends every Wednesday at the local centre for homeless people, chatting with them, and giving them a meal. She wants them to know God loves them, and they are her friends.

Helen goes to church every week. She thinks the vicar is boring, the organist is past it and everyone else very common. But she likes to go and admire the flowers she has arranged.

Tim goes to church every week. He loves God and does his best to live God's way. He has a bad temper but is working hard to learn to control it.

John goes to church every week. He sings in the choir. He refuses to speak to his sister and is secretly stealing money from the office.

To pray this week

Lord, I want to show my love and thanks in the way I live my life.
I want everything I think, say and do to be in line with your Law of love.
Lord, help me to be more concerned with the state of my soul before you than with my efforts to impress other people.
—Amen—

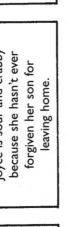
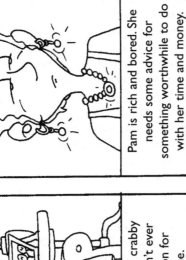
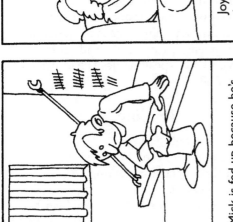

PROPER 18

Sunday between 4 and 10 September inclusive

Thought for the day

Jesus comes fulfilling the hope of healing to wholeness; he shows that mercy has triumphed over judgement.

Readings

Proverbs 22:1-2, 8-9, 22-23 or Isaiah 35:4-7a
Psalm 125 or Psalm 146
James 2:1-10 (11-13) 14-17
Mark 7:24-37

Aim

To know the healing events of today's Gospel.

Starter

Give out some instruments for some of the children to play and ask the others to close and open their ears so they can feel what it is like to be shut off from the sounds. Swap the instruments around so the others can have a go.

Teaching

Today we are going to hear about someone who couldn't hear anything at all, and he couldn't speak either. When he was trying to listen to someone, this is what it sounded like: (mime the words, but let no sound come out). Sometimes he could tell that people wanted him to do something but it was hard to work out what. (Mime the words 'please can you get me a chair' several times, getting more irritated as no one gets it, gradually adding gestures to help them understand.) People helped him as much as they could but it still felt very lonely being unable to hear. Sometimes he would see people saying something to each other and laughing, but he didn't get the joke as he couldn't hear the words. He hoped they weren't laughing about him.

One day his family said to him: (only mime the words) 'We're taking you to Jesus. He can make your ears better.' (Say it several times with increasing actions till they work it out.) The man was very pleased. He had seen Jesus before and thought he looked kind. Of course he hadn't been able to hear what Jesus had been saying but he had seen how interested the crowds were and how carefully they listened. He had even seen Jesus put his hands on people with eyes and legs that didn't work, and watched them shouting and laughing as they were made better. He could hardly wait to go to Jesus himself.

His family took him to where Jesus was, pushed through the crowd and said to Jesus (mime it only), 'Please, Jesus . . . put your hands . . . on him and make his ears better.' The man saw them speaking and worked out what they were saying, just as you have done. He watched Jesus nod and look straight at him, smiling. The man smiled back and tried to say, 'Hello, Jesus', but he couldn't speak so just some sounds came out. Jesus led the man away from all the people to be with him on his own. The man watched as Jesus put his fingers into the man's ears. He could feel them there but couldn't hear anything, like we usually do. Then Jesus spat and touched the man's tongue. Doctors at that time quite often used saliva in healing so to them this was quite an ordinary thing to do.

Now the really exciting bit happened. The man watched Jesus looking up to heaven and praying (mime only), 'Be opened! Be opened! Be opened!' Suddenly the man realised he had just *heard* what Jesus was saying, as well as *seen* what he said! He could hear everything, and a very noisy world it was, too. He could hear the birds all screeching and singing, the crowd in the distance, the leaves rattling in the wind and everything. The man started to say, 'Oh good heavens, I can hear!' And suddenly he heard his own voice speaking. Jesus had healed his speaking as well!

Praying

Father God, we want to pray
for all the people who can't hear properly.
We pray for those who are working
to mend their hearing
and making hearing aids to help them hear better.
Amen.

Activities

The sheet is arranged like a computer page, so that they can help create a web site about the man who was given his hearing and speech by Jesus.

Notes

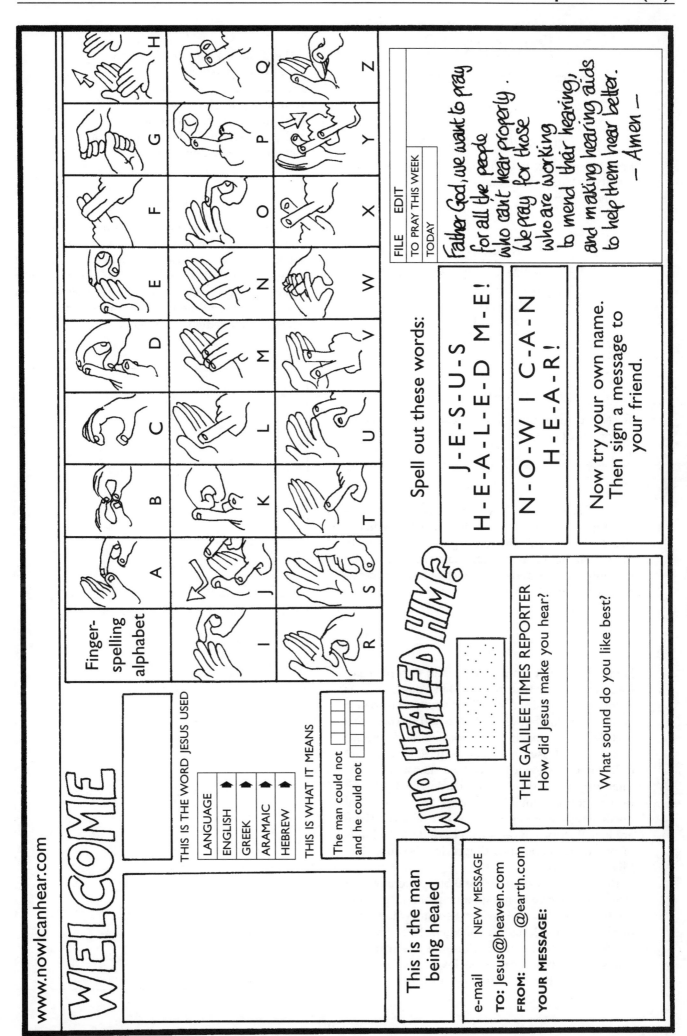

www.nowIcanhear.com

WELCOME

Finger-spelling alphabet

A B C D E F G H
I J K L M N O P
Q R S T U V W X
Y Z

THIS IS THE WORD JESUS USED

LANGUAGE	
ENGLISH	◆
GREEK	◆
ARAMAIC	◆
HEBREW	◆

THIS IS WHAT IT MEANS

The man could not ☐☐☐☐
and he could not ☐☐☐☐

This is the man being healed

e-mail   NEW MESSAGE

TO: Jesus@heaven.com

FROM: _____@earth.com

YOUR MESSAGE:

Spell out these words:

J-E-S-U-S
H-E-A-L-E-D M-E!

N-O-W I C-A-N
H-E-A-R!

Now try your own name.
Then sign a message to your friend.

WHO HEALED HIM?

THE GALILEE TIMES REPORTER
How did Jesus make you hear?

What sound do you like best?

FILE   EDIT
TO PRAY THIS WEEK
TODAY

Father God, we want to pray for all the people who can't hear properly. We pray for those who are working to mend their hearing, and making hearing aids to help them hear better.
— Amen —

Proper 19

Thought for the day

Loving obedience to God is shown by Jesus to be a quality rich in courage and wisdom, a quality to be highly respected.

Readings

Proverbs 1:20-33 or Isaiah 50:4-9a
Psalm 19 or Wisdom of Solomon 7:26-8:1 or
Psalm 116:1-9
James 3:1-12
Mark 8:27-38

Aim

To see the importance and value of Jesus' (and our) loving obedience.

Starter

Dogs and owners. Everyone gets into pairs, and takes it in turns to be the dog and its owner at obedience classes. They are all directed to get their pet to walk to heel, sit, lie down, beg and stay. They are told to give lots of praise and encouragement to their pet as soon at it obeys the instruction.

Teaching

Some of the children may have had experience of training a pet or watching working dogs, such as sheepdogs or police dogs. There always has to be a good friendship between the dog and its owner, so that the dog is obeying and working hard because it wants to please the owner it loves. How is that different from a dog who is badly treated and beaten? That just makes the dog crouch down frightened, or it might turn round and attack the owner. Real obedience is working together out of love. There are lots of stories of dogs who have done all kinds of brave and dangerous things, just because they love their owners.

Read Isaiah 50:4-5 from the Bible, preferably in a clear children's version, explaining that the prophet is talking about God's obedient Servant, who turned out to be Jesus. Jesus was obedient to everything the Father told him, not because he was scared of punishment, but because he loved his heavenly Father so much.

Praying

Father God, we want to obey you
because we love you,
and know that you love us.
Your loving kindness
is all around us in this world
and we choose to come to you and say,
'Let your will be done in us.'

Activities

The children will need access to a Bible for looking up references which give examples of Jesus' loving obedience, and they can also make a communal collage entitled, 'Let your kingdom come, let your will be done on earth as it is in heaven.' Help them to see that every time we pray this we are placing ourselves in obedience to God.

Notes

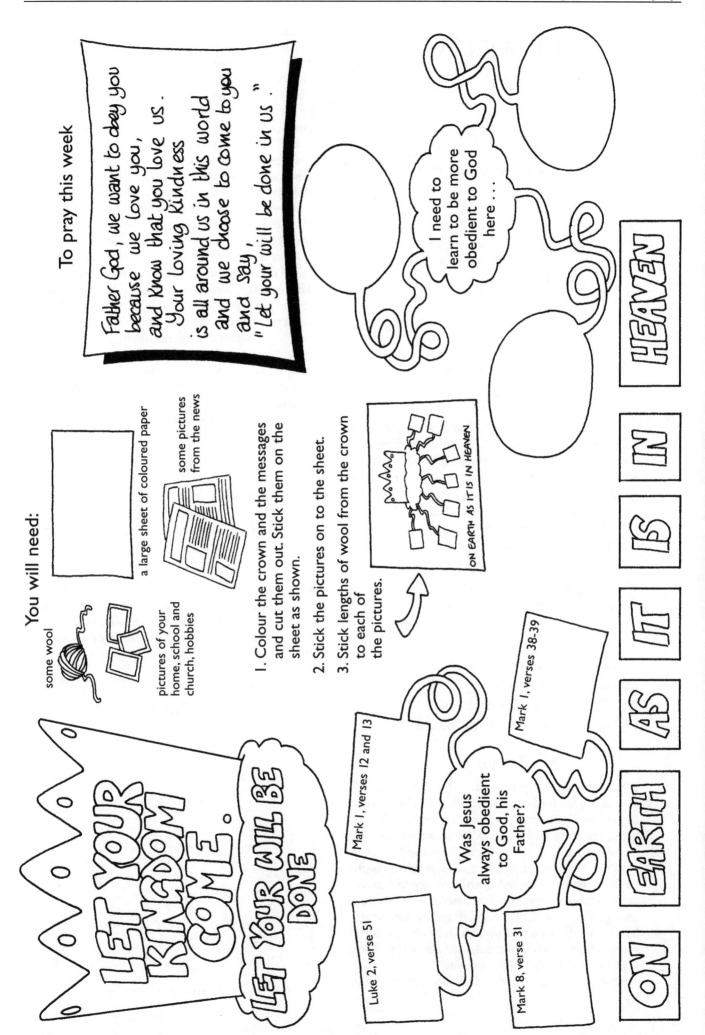

PROPER 20

Thought for the day

The truly great in God's eyes are those who are prepared to be last of all and servant of all.

Readings

Proverbs 31:10-31 or Wisdom of Solomon 1:16-2:1,
12-22 or Jeremiah 11:18-20
Psalm 1 or Psalm 54
James 3:13-4:3, 7-8a
Mark 9:30-37

Aim

To know about Jesus teaching the disciples that being servants is the way of true greatness.

Starter

VIP spaghetti quiz. Have a pot with some different length pieces of string in it. Split the children into teams, and ask the questions. If a question is answered correctly, that team takes a piece of spaghetti. At the end of the quiz, each team ties its pieces of spaghetti together. The longest wins. Here are some ideas for questions:

1. Who is the Prime Minister of England?
2. Who is the Headteacher of (school)?
3. Who is the rector of (church)?
4. Who is the captain of Liverpool?
5. Who is number one in the charts this week?
6. Who runs the Brownies here?
7. Who invented the telephone?
8. Which king had six wives?
9. Who plays (part) in (soap)?
10. Who introduces (animal programme)?

Teaching

What makes some people important and famous? Talk this over, looking at such things as being rich, clever, good-looking, speaking for the rest of us, being specially bad or good. What about God – if he was to draw up a list of important people, would it look the same? What kind of things might God be more concerned with? You could remind them of what happened when Samuel was choosing a king from Jesse's sons – God didn't go for the tall, handsome ones but the youngest, in charge of the sheep. People look at the outward appearance, but God looks at the heart of a person.

One day some of Jesus' disciples were walking along the road having a bit of an argument. Was it about who had to do the washing-up? No. Was it about something Jesus had been teaching them? No. Was it about the road they needed to take? No. They were arguing about which of them ought to be the most important – the greatest of the disciples. Perhaps it went something like this. (Give out different 'scripts' to various children who can read.) Perhaps Peter was saying . . . (Peter reads out: 'I am best. I am very good at fishing. Jesus likes my fish.') Perhaps Andrew was saying . . . (Andrew reads out: 'I am best. I was one of the first to be called by Jesus.') Perhaps James was saying . . . (James reads out: 'I am best. My name starts with a J and so does Jesus.')

They all had their reasons for thinking they ought to be the greatest, most important disciple of all. That evening, Jesus asked them what they had been arguing about, and they all felt rather silly. It didn't seem to matter who was best when Jesus was there. But Jesus wanted to teach them something very important. And it's important for us to learn as well, because we are all Jesus' followers. Jesus explained that the way to be greatest in the kingdom of God was to be the last of all and the servant of all! Not richest, not best-looking, not sporting champion, but the last of all and the servant of all.

Praying

Lord, teach me the joy
of serving others for no reward
apart from knowing that I am making you happy.

Activities

On the sheet there is a maze to construct and follow. All the usual worldly status symbols turn out to be dead ends, but the right route is going by the way of loving service. They will need thin card to reinforce the bottom of the maze and the uprights.

Notes

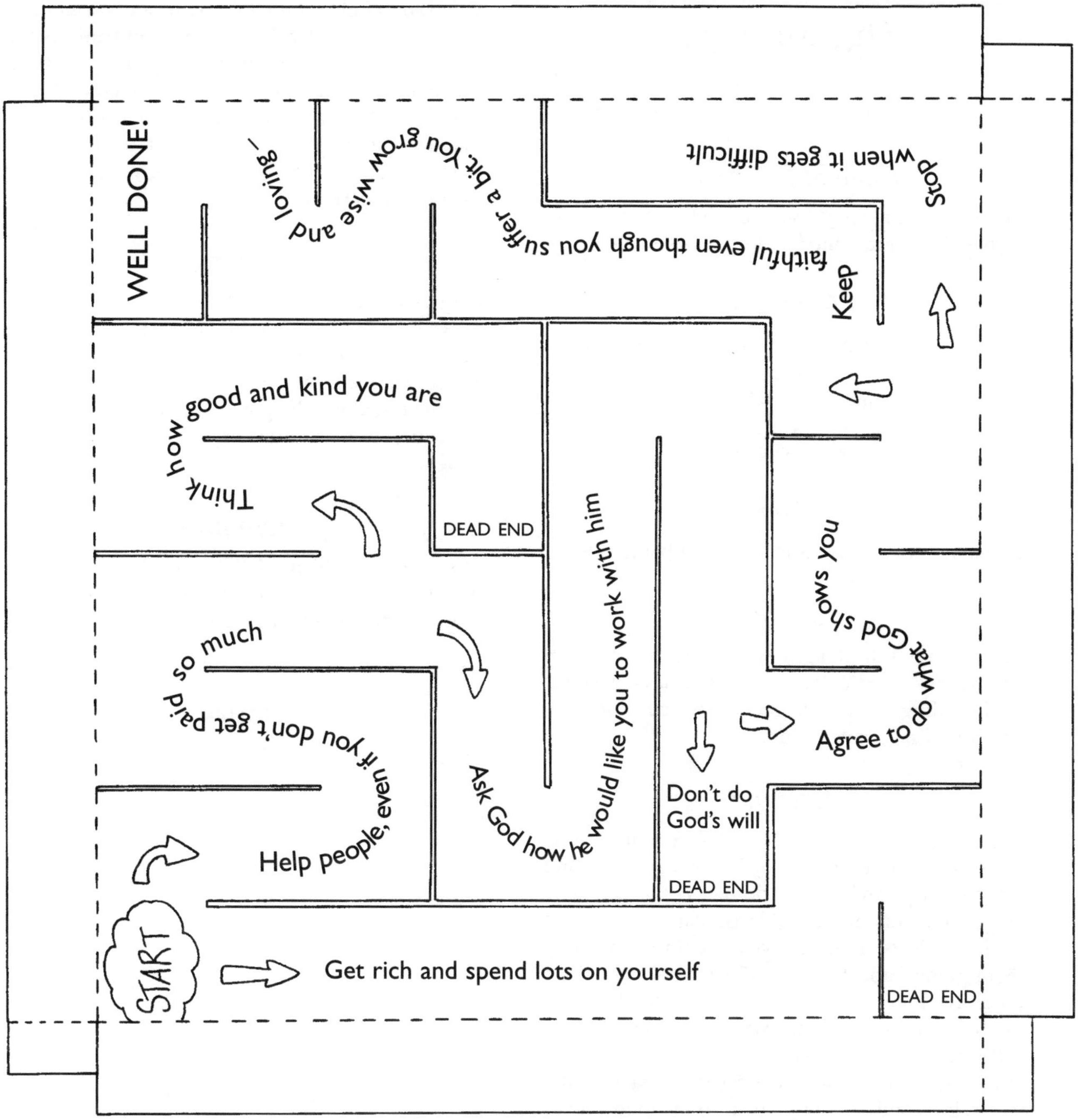
START
Get rich and spend lots on yourself
DEAD END
Help people, even if you don't get paid so much
Think how good and kind you are
DEAD END
Ask God how he would like you to work with him
Don't do God's will
DEAD END
Agree to do what God shows you
Keep faithful even though you suffer a bit. You grow wise and loving –
Stop when it gets difficult
WELL DONE!

To pray this week

Lord, teach me the joy of serving others for no reward apart from knowing that I am making you happy.

HOW TO MAKE YOUR AMAZING! MAZE

Sellotape thin card walls along the wall lines and stick the sheet on to thin card as well.
Bend up the edges and stick them together, like this:

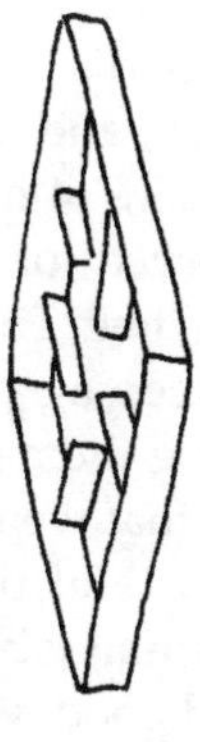

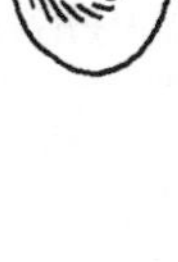

Use a marble and pretend it's you!

PROPER 21

Sunday between 25 September and 1 October inclusive

Thought for the day

Don't let your body lead you into sin and risk exchanging eternal life for eternal punishment.

Readings

Esther 7:1-6, 9-10; 9:20-22 or Numbers 11:4-6, 10-16, 24-29

Psalm 124 or Psalm 19:7-14

James 5:13-20

Mark 9:38-50

Aim

To get to know Jesus' teaching about being salt.

Starter

Make some salt dough, with different children adding the ingredients and everyone having a go at the kneading. Here is the recipe: two cups of flour, one cup of salt, water to mix.

Teaching

Put on display some cubes of Cheddar cheese, some small pieces of ham or bacon, some salt and vinegar crisps and the salt dough. What have they all got in common? Salt! (Place a salt pot down as well.) Salt is used to preserve these things and stop them going bad. It was used a lot for this where Jesus lived and so Jesus used it as a good way to teach his disciples about what they (and we) are called to do in this world.

He tells us to be salt! Just as cheese, soaked in salty water, lasts and doesn't go bad, so the followers of Jesus are to be like salt to the world, stopping people from getting ruined and lost for ever by going bad. What would 'going bad' mean for people? It means thinking and doing what is wrong and evil and against God's way of goodness, truth and love. That is sin, and sin leads towards hell. Hell is like the opposite of heaven, and Jesus wants people to be preserved, or kept alive to God, so they don't end up in hell. That's why he needs us to work with him at keeping people alive to God for ever, and preserving them from evil.

To do that we need to be salty salt! Let everyone have a taste of the cheese, crisps and ham. To do our Christian job of preserving, or keeping people fresh and good, we need to make sure that we keep our own lives free from sin. Otherwise we'd all end up going bad! Sometimes temptations to do the wrong thing are really strong, and hard to fight off.

We need to fight temptation with God's armour on, and with God's weapons of love and truth, prayer and praise. It's a battle, fighting temptation, but God's power is stronger than evil, so if we stick with God, we'll win. And if we do fall into sin, it's important that we sort things out with God as soon as we possibly can, so that God can forgive us and help us put things right.

Praying

Forgive us our sins
as we forgive those who sin against us.
Lead us not into temptation
but set us free from evil.
For the kingdom, the power and the glory
are yours for ever and ever.
Amen.

Activities

The children will need Bibles to do the activities based on Mark 9 and James 5, and some salt dough to make the models suggested.

Notes

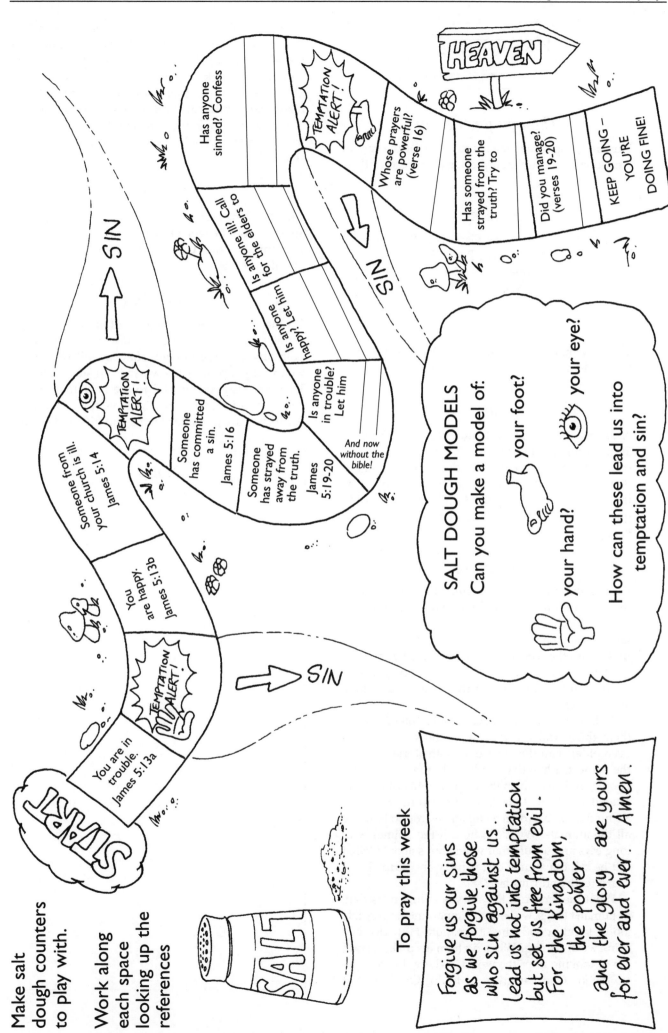

PROPER 22

Sunday between 2 and 8 October inclusive

Thought for the day

Human beings are made responsible for the care of creation but are subject to God in all aspects of their lives.

Readings

Job 1:1; 2:1-10 or Genesis 2:18-24
Psalm 26 or Psalm 8
Hebrews 1:1-4; 2:5-12
Mark 10:2-16

Aim

To know that we are responsible for looking after the world and under God's authority.

Starter

Name the animal. Have a number of pictures of animals spread out on the floor or wall so everyone can see them. One person decides on an animal but doesn't say which it is. This person starts to describe the animal, one fact at a time, and the others try to guess which one it is. Whoever names it first has next go.

Teaching

Explain that the Bible has included two versions of the story of how the world was made, one an even older story than the other. Show them the story we know best, the one at the very beginning of the Bible, with the world being made stage by stage, in six days, or ages. Adam and Eve – the first people – were made on day six, and they were told to look after the world.

Today's reading is from Genesis chapter 2. (Show them this.) And this version of the same story is even older than the other one. Both stories give us the same truth – that God made the world, and people, and gave them the responsibility of looking after it all. Read today's reading from the Bible. Remind them of Adam being taken around to name all the animals. What did he call the animal with long ears and a fluffy tail which hops about? What did he call the animal that is furry and striped, has sharp teeth and runs fast?

What the writer of the story is telling us is that, as human beings, we have the important, responsible job of taking good care of creation. How do they think we are doing? When do humans make a good job of looking after the world? Where do we mess up the job God has given us to do? On a sheet of paper or a blackboard, jot down their ideas in tick and cross columns. Talk through any ideas they have for ways we could do better, locally and internationally. (Look, for instance, at recycling our litter, asking for simpler packaging, using feet and bikes and public transport more instead of cars.)

We have to look after one another as well – our friends and the people in our families. How? Again, share ideas.

Praying

All good gifts around us
are sent from heaven above;
so thank the Lord, O thank the Lord,
for all his love!

Activities

On the sheet there are pictures of animals nearing extinction, forests being cut down and industry polluting the environment. They can talk over what we can do to protect the world from such damage. They are also encouraged to see how they might help others in the world who have no fresh water. Addresses are given for letters and gifts to be sent.

Notes

PROPER 23

Sunday between 9 and 15 October inclusive

Thought for the day

The word of God is living and active, piercing right to the heart; only with God is it possible to be saved.

Readings

Job 23:1-9, 16-17 or Amos 5:6-7, 10-15
Psalm 22:1-15 or Psalm 90:12-17
Hebrews 4:12-16
Mark 10:17-31

Aim

To know the story of the rich young man, and Jesus' teaching about entering the kingdom.

Starter

Creeping with the keys. Sit in a circle, with one person in the centre, blindfolded. Someone is given a bunch of keys, and they creep all round the outside of the circle, trying to get back in and to the person in the middle without being heard. If the blindfolded person hears the keys, she points in the direction of the sound. If that is the right place, she joins the circle and someone else becomes blindfolded in the centre. (Nice peaceful game, this!)

Teaching

God is never blindfolded – he sees everything. Sometimes people creep around the world doing what they know is evil and wrong, thinking that God can't see and doesn't know, but God knows all about their evil, and he knows why they are doing it. So God can see everything about us – both our outsides and our innermost secret thoughts. But we can't see God, can we? That's because God is Spirit, and so bright with goodness and love that we wouldn't be able to cope with seeing him just yet. But he does want us to seek for him, searching him out so that we get to know him really well. Today we're going to hear about someone who was seeking God for all he was worth.

You will need two of the leaders, two of the young people, or a leader and a rehearsed child to prepare the script on page 134. The actors can be dressed up.

Praying

It's so hard to enter the kingdom of God
but I want so much to do it;
harder than threading a camel through a needle,
but I want so much to be there.
Your kingdom of love and joy and peace
is the place I want to be,
and I know that only through God my Saviour
can I enter it and be free!
Amen.

Activities

The sheet can be made into a card which enables us to get into the kingdom through the grace of God. They will need a Bible to work out the puzzle about the word of God.

Notes

112

Q. How can we get into the kingdom of God?
A. Through 1 2 3 4 – that's the only way!

Find Hebrews 4:12-16

God's word is a 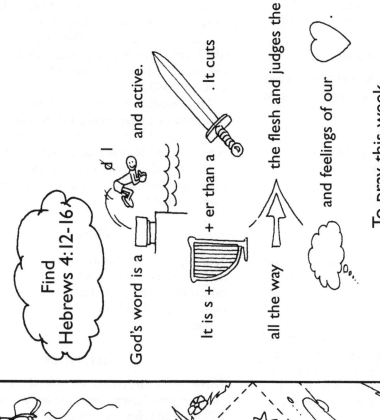 and active.

It is s + er than a . It cuts all the way the flesh and judges the and feelings of our .

To pray this week

It's so hard to enter the Kingdom of God but I want so much to do it; harder than threading a camel through a needle, but I want so much to be there. Your Kingdom of love and joy and peace is the place I want to be, and I know that only through God my saviour can I enter it and be free! —Amen—

Write 1 on the back

Write 2 on the back

GRACE
THE
KINGDOM
OF
GOD

Write 3 on the back

Write 4 on the back

PROPER 24

Sunday between 16 and 22 October inclusive

Thought for the day

Even the Son of Man himself came not to be served but to serve, and to give his life as a ransom for many.

Readings

Job 38:1-7 (34-41) or Isaiah 53:4-12
Psalm 104:1-9, 24, 35c or Psalm 91:9-16
Hebrews 5:1-10
Mark 10:35-45

Aim

To know the story of John and James' question, and Jesus' teaching about servanthood in leadership.

Starter

Write out a set of questions and a set of answers, all on different pieces of card. Spread them around and turn them blank side up, so the children can play pairs with them, turning over any two at a time and keeping them if they match. Only one go each in a round.

Ideas for questions:

- What are the colours of the rainbow?
- How far is the sun from the earth?
- What two colours make purple?
- Why is it dangerous to look straight at the sun?
- What is steel made of?
- How fast can leopards run?
- What are the seasons called?
- Which month comes straight after July?
- What is the capital city of France?
- When was the battle of Hastings?

Teaching

Who learnt something from that game which they didn't know before? We all learn by asking questions, and anyone with younger brothers and sisters will know that they are always asking, 'Why?' Sometimes we ask questions which are so difficult that we can't understand the answers. (Perhaps like our question of how far away the sun is from the earth.) It's good to ask questions all through our lives.

One day, two of Jesus' disciples, John and James, asked Jesus a question which he couldn't answer. It wasn't because the question was too hard, but because it was the sort of question that shouldn't have been asked in the first place. And this was it (have it written out large and clear for everyone to read): 'Can one of us sit at your right hand and the other at your left in your glory?'

What had Jesus been trying to show his disciples about the way to live? (Collect their ideas, writing them down on a sheet titled: 'If you want to be my followers you must . . .' They might include things like loving one another, loving God, looking after one another, being the servant of all and trying to do God's will.)

That question of James and John shows that they hadn't really understood this teaching yet, had they? They were still interested in how important they would be and how much respect they could expect.

What do they think Jesus might have said to that question? Share ideas and then read it in the passage from Mark 10.

Praying

Take my love; my Lord, I pour
at thy feet its treasure-store;
take myself, and I will be
ever, only, all for thee.
Amen.

Activities

There are instructions on the sheet for making another 'pairs' game, based on Jesus' teaching. They will need to colour the sheet, mount it on card, and cut the cards out.

Notes

a pairs game to make

1. Colour the cards
2. Stick the whole sheet on card
3. Cut out the cards

Mark 1:35
Jesus got up early and went to a quiet place to pray.

Luke 22:19
'This is my body, given for you. Do this in memory of me.'

Matthew 25:37-40
'Lord, when did we see you thirsty and give you a drink?'
'Whatever you did for one of the least of these you did for me.'

NO CLIMBING

Matthew 5:7
'Blessed are the merciful, for they will be shown mercy.'

Mark 6:37
But he answered, 'You give them something to eat.'

Matthew 5:16
'Let your light shine so people see the good you do and it points them to God.'

Matthew 18:5
'Whoever welcomes a little child like this in my name, welcomes me.'

John 13:14
'You are to wash one another's feet.'

To pray this week

Take my love; my Lord I pour at your feet its treasure-store; take myself, and I will be ever, only, all for thee. — Amen —

Proper 25

Sunday between 23 and 29 October inclusive

Thought for the day

In Jesus, God gathers his scattered people and opens their eyes to see.

Readings

Job 42:1-6, 10-17 or Jeremiah 31:7-9
Psalm 34:1-8, 19-22 or Psalm 126
Hebrews 7:23-28
Mark 10:46-52

Aim

To look at what we can learn from the way Bartimaeus is healed.

Starter

Blindfold everybody and stand them all over the room. Ask everyone to move about, and, when they find someone else, to hold hands and go on together, till they find someone else to join up with. When you can see that everyone is joined up together, tell everyone to freeze and open their eyes. They will be surprised to find that they are all linked up.

Teaching

We are all going to act today's Gospel. Get to know the Gospel account really well, so that you can narrate it, directing various children to do the actions as they happen.

Put up a sign which says 'To Jericho' and choose someone to be Bartimaeus. Direct them to sit by the roadside and give them a begging bowl to hold. Bartimaeus is blindfolded. Choose someone to be Jesus and two others to be disciples. Gather the crowd at Jericho and explain that we are all following Jesus, who has been teaching and healing in the town.

All the crowd are walking on the spot. We're just leaving the city, and Bartimaeus can hear us coming, so he's shouting out at the top of his voice, 'Jesus, son of David, have mercy on me!' Now a few people are going ahead, trying to make the blind man be quiet. But the man is shouting even louder, the same thing again. This time Jesus stops, and we all stop as well. Jesus tells the disciples to call the blind man. They go over to him and cheer him up, telling him that Jesus is calling him. The blind man jumps up, not bothering to pick up his cloak, and comes across to Jesus. (The disciples might well be guiding him.)

Jesus says to Bartimaeus, 'What do you want me to do for you?' Bartimaeus says to Jesus, 'Teacher, I want to see.' Jesus says to him, 'Go, your faith has healed you,' and suddenly the man finds he can see. (Jesus helps him to take off the blindfold.) The crowd moves off down the road, very happy for the man, and Bartimaeus is walking with Jesus, looking around at things for the first time ever.

Praying

Jesus, you made the blind to see,
open my eyes to see your love.
Jesus, you made the deaf to hear,
open my ears to hear your truth.
All we need we find in you;
your love is total, your words are true.

Activities

On the sheet they are taken through the story of the Gospel stage by stage, with questions which help them deepen their understanding of how God works in our lives and in our needs. They will need a Bible to help them with this.

Notes

Do we help people to meet Jesus or not?

Why do you think the man wants to follow Jesus?

What is it called when we ask Jesus for help?

What do you want to thank Jesus for?

Mark 10:46-52. How are people who can see, sometimes blind

Who do you know who needs Jesus' healing?

How often does Jesus hear us when we pray?

To pray this week

Jesus, you made the blind to see,
open my eyes to see your love.
Jesus, you made the deaf to hear,
open my ears to hear your truth.
All we need we find in you;
your love is total,
your words are true.

ALL SAINTS' DAY

Sunday between 30 October and 5 November inclusive

Thought for the day

Great is the rejoicing in heaven among the saints of God as they worship their Lord in glory.

Readings

Wisdom 3:1-9 or Isaiah 25:6-9
Psalm 24:1-6
Revelation 21:1-6a
John 11:32-44

Aim

To become familiar with some of the descriptions of heaven in the Bible.

Starter

Pass the halo. Use a shampoo shield and put on some music. Pass the halo round. The one wearing it when the music stops is out, folding their arms in the circle to show this. Carry on till only one or two are left and give them a small prize.

Teaching

Describe a picture to the children and ask them to imagine it. Then show them the picture. It's always quite hard to describe something so that we know exactly what it's like. Sometimes it's better to describe what it feels like than what it looks like. Someone could try describing what it feels like to be lost and then found again. Someone else could try describing what it feels like to be really tired after a hard match and come home to a shower and your favourite meal.

Today we are celebrating all the saints who have lived and struggled through this life, just as we are now, and they were such close friends of Jesus that he was able to do amazing work through them. When they died and came into the presence of God, it must have been a little like coming home to a hot shower and our favourite meal after a long, hard match. They were given a great welcome in heaven, like a wonderful homecoming. We're going to listen to some people describing it.

Put on some quiet, gentle music and read Wisdom 3:1-5, 7-9, Revelation 21:3-4, and Psalm 24:3-5.

Today we are thanking God for the way these people lived. Now they cheer us on as we walk through our lifetimes, as Jesus' friends. And one day, we hope to join that great party in heaven!

Praying

You spread a banquet for me
in the presence of my enemies;
my head you have anointed with oil
and my cup is overflowing.
Surely goodness and kindness shall follow me
all the days of my life,
and I shall live in the house of the Lord for ever.

(From Psalm 23)

Activities

The sheet can be made into a stained-glass window. The children will need some coloured cellophane or tissue paper, or they can colour the window with coloured pencils and then dab cooking oil over it to make it translucent. (Rest the sheets on newspapers for this.)

Notes

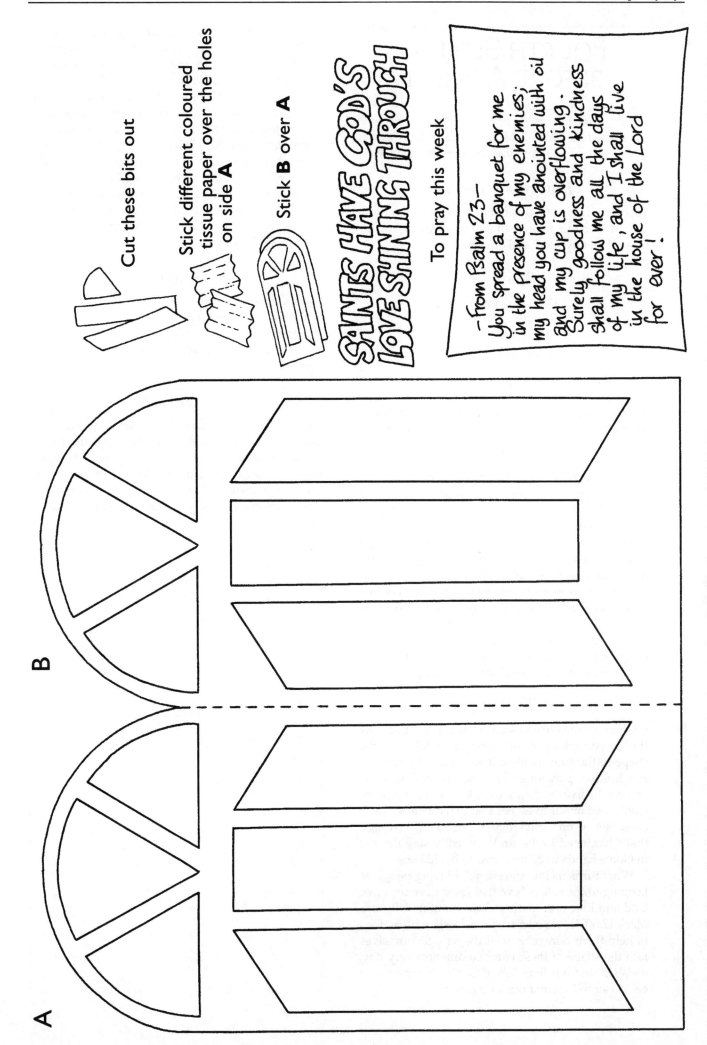

Cut these bits out

Stick different coloured tissue paper over the holes on side **A**

Stick **B** over **A**

SAINTS HAVE GOD'S LOVE SHINING THROUGH

To pray this week

—from Psalm 23—
You spread a banquet for me
in the presence of my enemies;
my head you have anointed with oil
and my cup is overflowing.
Surely goodness and kindness
shall follow me all the days
of my life, and I shall live
in the house of the Lord
for ever!

B

A

Fourth Sunday before Advent

Sunday between 30 October and 5 November inclusive*

* For use if the Feast of All Saints was celebrated on 1 November and alternative propers are needed

Thought for the day

To love the living God with heart, soul and strength, and to love our neighbour as ourselves means far more than any sacrificial offerings.

Readings

Deuteronomy 6:1-9
Psalm 119:1-8
Hebrews 9:11-14
Mark 12:28-34

Aim

To know about the scribe's question and Jesus' answer.

Starter

Have some playdough and a number of different shapes to press the dough into so that they mould it. Ideas for shapes: shells, lids, buttons, shortbread moulds, coins.

Here is a recipe for playdough. Mix two teaspoons of cream of tartar, one cup of plain flour, half a cup of salt, one tablespoon of oil and one cup of water to form a smooth paste. Cook slowly in a saucepan until the dough comes away from the sides of the pan and forms a ball. When the dough is cool enough, take it out of the pan, add food colouring and knead for three or four minutes. (Store in an airtight container in the fridge.)

Teaching

Look at all the created shapes, and point out how the playdough was soft enough to take on the shape of the firm moulds. If we think of ourselves as a lump of playdough (!), then having God's law of love to live by helps us take on the shape of God's love in our lives. For that to happen we can't be so set in our ways that we're like playdough that's hardened in the air. We need to stay flexible in God's hands to be moulded to his likeness.

What turns us into the shape of loving people is keeping to the rule of love that Jesus gave us: Love God and love one another. Read it out in full from Mark 12:30-31. Go over it again slowly with actions to help them remember it. If we wriggle ourselves into the shape of those commandments every day, we shall find our lives full of God's blessing as we get closer to him and our love grows.

One day when Jesus was teaching and answering people's questions, a scribe came and asked him what was the first among all the commandments. As a scribe, he would have studied the scriptures and God's law very thoroughly. He wasn't trying to trick Jesus, but really wanted to understand God better. Jesus answered the scribe by quoting the scriptures to him, which he knew well, and showing him what they really meant. They weren't really about rules at all but about loving God!

The scribe could see how right that was, and this is what he said: (read Mark 12:32-33). And Jesus was happy for the scribe and told him he was close to the kingdom of God.

Praying

Lord, we pray for those
who don't yet know you.
We pray that they will find you
and discover how lovely you are.
Amen.

Activities

On the sheet the children learn about the sacrifices offered by the priests, so that they can better understand the scribe's concern to get back to real, heartfelt worship, rather than going through the motions. They are encouraged to say the Lord's prayer every day, thinking carefully about the words as they say them.

Notes

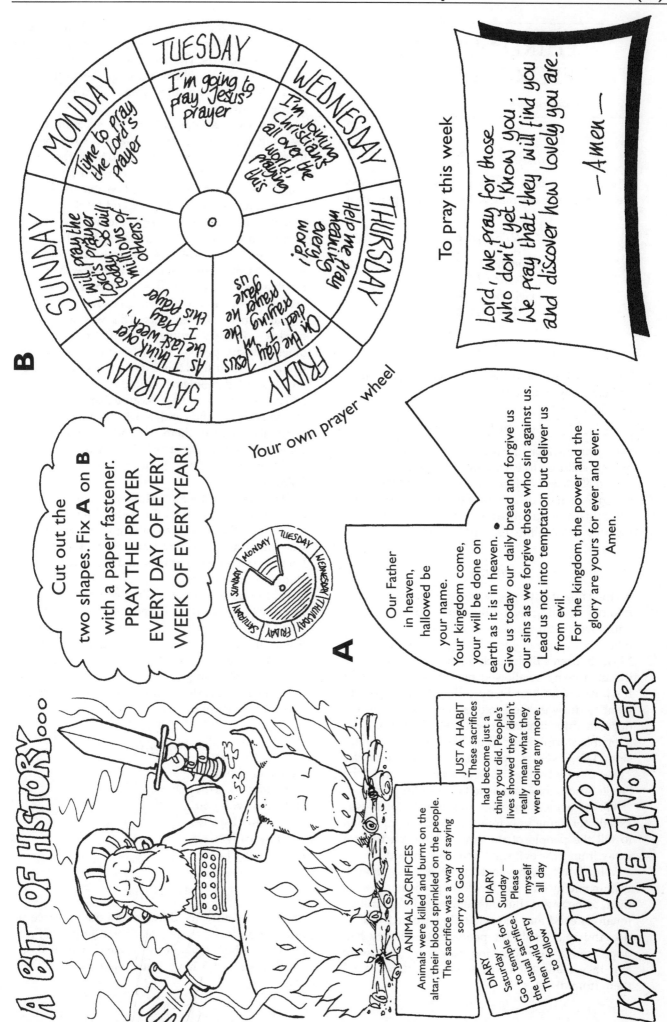

B

MONDAY — Time to pray the Lord's prayer

TUESDAY — I'm going to pray Jesus' prayer

WEDNESDAY — I'm joining Christians all over the world praying this

THURSDAY — Help me pray meaning every word!

FRIDAY — On the day Jesus died, I'm praying the prayer he gave us

SATURDAY — As I think over the last week, I pray this prayer

SUNDAY — I will pray the Lord's prayer today. So will millions of others!

Your own prayer wheel

To pray this week

Lord, we pray for those who don't yet know you. We pray that they will find you and discover how lovely you are. — Amen —

Cut out the two shapes. Fix **A** on **B** with a paper fastener. PRAY THE PRAYER EVERY DAY OF EVERY WEEK OF EVERY YEAR!

A

Our Father in heaven, hallowed be your name. Your kingdom come, your will be done on earth as it is in heaven. Give us today our daily bread and forgive us our sins as we forgive those who sin against us. Lead us not into temptation but deliver us from evil. For the kingdom, the power and the glory are yours for ever and ever. Amen.

A BIT OF HISTORY...

ANIMAL SACRIFICES
Animals were killed and burnt on the altar, their blood sprinkled on the people. The sacrifice was a way of saying sorry to God.

JUST A HABIT
These sacrifices had become just a thing you did. People's lives showed they didn't really mean what they were doing any more.

DIARY —
Saturday for temple.
Go to sacrifice.
the usual wild party
Then follow

DIARY
Sunday —
Please myself all day

LOVE GOD, LOVE ONE ANOTHER

THIRD SUNDAY
BEFORE ADVENT

Sunday between 6 and 12 November inclusive

Thought for the day

When we are called we need to respond with obedience so that many may be brought to repentance.

Readings

Jonah 3:1-5, 10
Psalm 62:5-12
Hebrews 9:24-28
Mark 1:14-20

Aim

To look at Jonah and the fishermen – being called and choosing to follow.

Starter

Have some water in washing-up bowls and three or four children to each bowl. Scatter some leaves and small sticks (such as spent matches) in the water and give each group a piece of the net which oranges come in from supermarkets. They have to work together to catch the 'fish' in the 'net'.

Teaching

As they might have guessed, some fishermen come into our teaching today! But we're not starting off with them; we're starting off with a very large fish. (Show a picture of Jonah being swallowed by it. Most children's Bibles include this picture.) Who is the man being swallowed by the enormous fish? It's Jonah, who heard God calling him and didn't want to do what God said, so he raced off in the opposite direction and got on a boat to Spain. After a terrible storm he ended up like this. Not a pretty sight. Did God give up on Jonah as a bad job? No! Three days later the fish spat Jonah out on to the beach. And once again he felt God calling him.

Was it a nicer message this time? No! It was exactly the same as before. God was calling Jonah to tell the people of the city of Nineveh to turn away from their evil ways and back to God.

Why didn't Jonah want to do it? Because Nineveh was an enemy city, and he didn't particularly want them to be saved. But this time when God called, Jonah listened and did what God wanted him to do. And as a result, the people realised they had done wrong, they told God how sorry they were and they really tried to do better. So God saved them from disaster.

So much for the big fish. Now back to the fishermen.

Andrew and Simon Peter were brothers. James and John were brothers. They all worked as fishermen on the sea of Galilee, which is a large, beautiful lake. And, just like Jonah, they were called by God. It happened like this.

Jesus was just starting out on his ministry of teaching and healing, and he needed some people to be his students. He was going to teach them over the next couple of years so that when he was no longer on the earth, they would be able to carry on his work in the world. Who would he choose? The religious teachers and leaders? No. Rich, powerful people who could get them into the posh places? No. Who then? Jesus watched the way the fishermen worked hard and stuck at it even when it was uncomfortable work. He saw their common sense and ordinariness, and the way they reached out for the fish and mended their nets. This was what Jesus needed – ordinary people who could talk to all the other ordinary people, and who knew what it was like to be exhausted after a day's work, and still go on. He wanted people who could reach out to others and knew about mending, because there are so many whose bodies, minds and spirits need mending.

So Jesus called them – 'Andrew and Simon, come and follow me. I will have you fishing for people instead of fish!' 'James and John, come and follow me!'

Did they do a Jonah and make excuses, or race off in their boats to the other side of the lake? No! They knew that God was calling them, and that it was important to follow Jesus. So they did. They left their boats and their nets, and set off to be Jesus' students, or disciples.

And Jesus still comes calling ordinary, practical people who can work hard, and talk to other ordinary people and help in their mending. Is he calling you? If you find he is, tell him in your prayer time that you are ready to do what he wants you to do, and then enjoy following wherever he leads you in your life. One thing's certain – you'll have an exciting life as one of Jesus' students!

Praying

Here I am, Lord,
ready to walk with you
and work with you.
I've got my L-plates
and I'm ready to go.
Lead on, my Lord!

Activities

There are pictures of different sounds to place in order of decibels, as they learn that Jesus' call can be very loud or very quiet. And they can read about some others who have heard God's call in their lives.

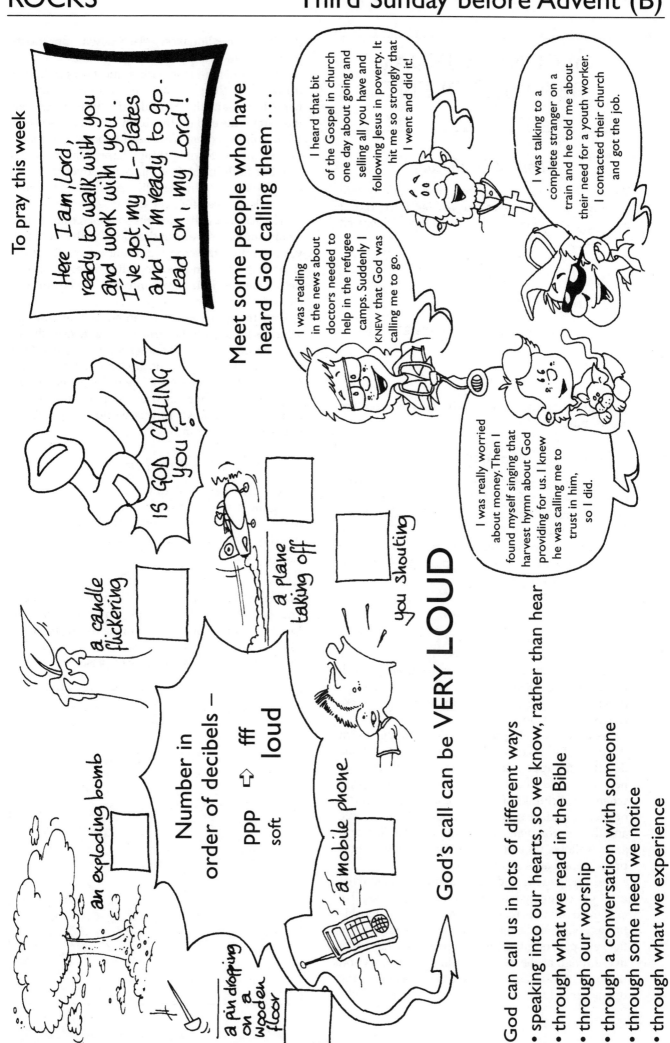

SECOND SUNDAY BEFORE ADVENT

Sunday between 13 and 19 November inclusive

Thought for the day

We are to be on our guard; great anguish will accompany the last days, but all that is good and loving, wise and true will be saved and celebrated for ever.

Readings

Daniel 12:1-3
Psalm 16
Hebrews 10:11-14 (15-18) 19-25
Mark 13:1-8

Aim

To begin to look at what the Bible tells us about the end of time.

Starter

Predicting the weather. Beforehand prepare a large notebook with different types of weather pictures on each page. (The pages need to be thick enough for the pictures not to show through.) Everyone takes a turn in giving the weather forecast for the next day, and then you turn the page to reveal what it really is, and so on.

Teaching

Predicting the weather in some countries is dead simple because it's nearly always the same. In other climate zones, the weather is very changeable, which makes it hard to predict. Like the weather, some things in life are pretty certain, while others are things we have no idea about.

Today we're going to look at something which none of us knows much about at all, except that one day it will happen. It's the end of the world. We hear and read about all kinds of horror stories, where great chunks of meteors crash into the earth, or there's a nuclear war which kills all the people and the environment, or the sun suddenly flares up and swallows up earth. (Place down a few appropriate paperbacks and film fliers.)

Jesus helped his students (and us) to look at what the end of everything might really be like. He explained that there will be all kinds of terrible things going on beforehand, just as we read about in the newspapers and many poor people are having to live through at the moment – things like wars and rumours of wars, famines where many people starve because they have no food, and natural disasters like floods and earthquakes. (Place down appropriate pictures from newspapers and magazines.)

(Place down a cross with a question mark over it.) Do these things mean the end of everything is here? Jesus says they are like the 'birth pains' but they aren't the end (or the 'birth') itself. Jesus warns all his followers that we'll need to be on our guard, in case all the terrible things happening make us lose our faith in the God of love. (Cover the cross completely with the terrible pictures.) The ones who will be saved for ever are those who keep their faith (clear away the pictures so the cross is visible again) and have lived out their lives with love (place your hand on the cross), guiding others along the right pathways, and looking after those who need help. That was Jesus' way, and that is to be our way as his followers.

One thing we are sure about is that nothing which is loving, kind or true is going to ever disappear, because God will gather it all up safely. That means that the people who are kind and loving and honest will the heroes and heroines at the end of time, whether they are rich or poor, famous or completely unknown in this world. All goodness gets a hero's welcome!

Praying

Lead me, Father, through this life,
along the pathway of your love.
May I keep to it, help others to find it, and,
one day, may it lead me straight into your heaven!

Activities

There is a 'Which lasts longest?' activity on the sheet, and the children will be making a model pathway of love that leads to heaven, following the instructions. They will each need a card base, and some modelling medium – which could be clay or plasticine.

Notes

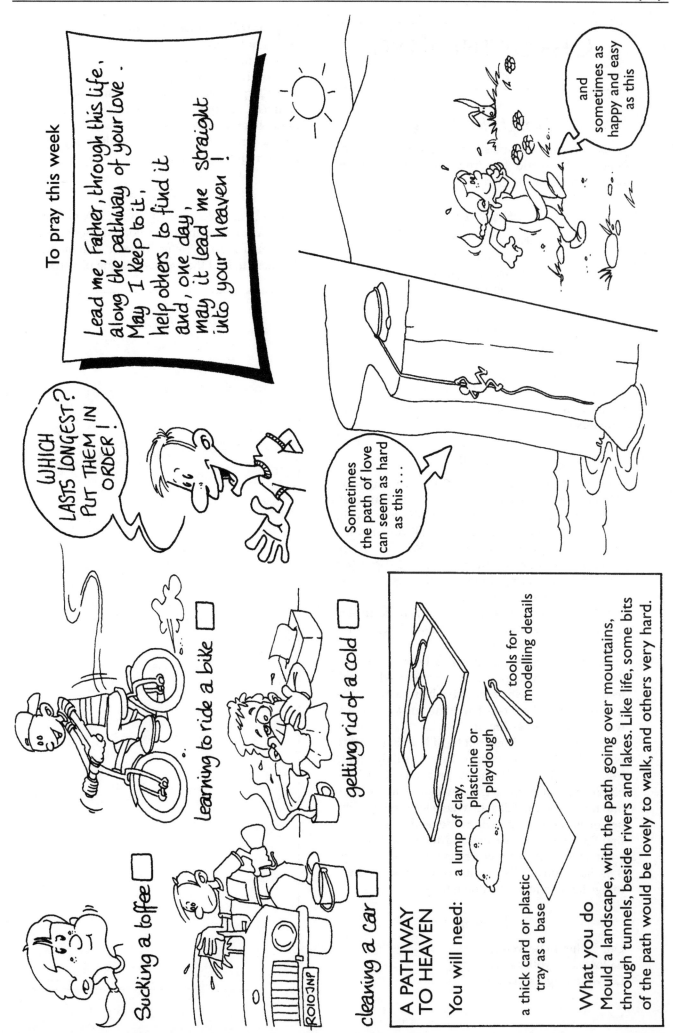

CHRIST THE KING

Sunday between 20 and 26 November inclusive

Thought for the day

Jesus Christ is the everlasting King whose kingdom is not of this world, but grows in the hearts of his people and lasts for ever.

Readings

Daniel 7:9-10, 13-14
Psalm 93
Revelation 1:4b-8
John 18:33-37

Aim

To look at the kind of king Jesus is.

Starter

Sit in a circle and share some of the dreams we remember.

Teaching

Give each child their sheet on which they can draw Daniel's dream as you read it to them. Can they work out who the 'son of man' is that Daniel saw in his vision? Explain that, as with all dreams, it's picture language. So why a throne? Why fire? They show us God's great power, and fire also purifies gold and silver, brings light into darkness and has to be treated with great respect.

What kind of king is Jesus shown to be in this dream? He's the King of all time and space, not for a little while but for ever.

Just before Jesus was crucified he was taken to Pilate, the Roman governor, who wanted to ask Jesus about him being accused of being a king. Was it true? Have the Gospel written out as a script, with two people reading it.

Yes, Jesus was a King, but he didn't have earthly power like Pilate, for instance. How was it different? Jesus reigns in people's hearts and souls. Our lives become his kingdom's territory when we invite Jesus into them. You can tell a life where Jesus reigns. The person is gradually growing wiser and more loving, finding it easier to forgive, and they find they are wanting to reach out to others and do good. Perhaps they have already begun to notice some of these things happening in their own lives.

Praying

Our Father in heaven,
hallowed be your name.
Let your kingdom come;
let your will be done on earth
as it is in heaven.
Give us today our daily bread
and forgive us our sins
as we forgive those who sin against us.
And lead us not into temptation
but deliver us from evil.
For the kingdom, the power and the glory are yours
for ever and ever. Amen.

Activities

They can complete their picture of Daniel's vision, cut it out and mount it on coloured paper beside the decorated Lord's Prayer. There is also an alphabet for them to find the names of some pictures.

Notes

ABCDEFGHIJKLMNOPQRSTUVWXYZ

Can you find these in the letters

Daniel's dream – based on Daniel 7:9-10, 13-14

To pray
this week

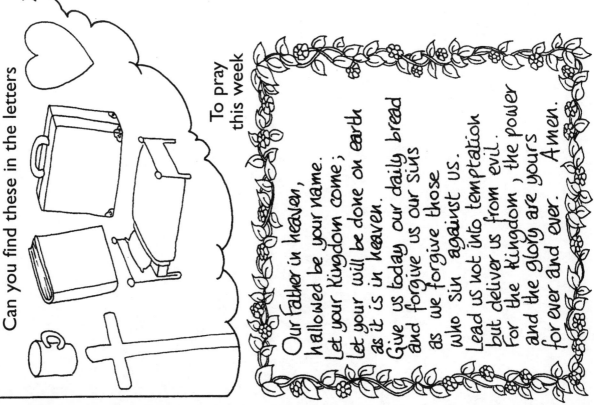

Our father in heaven,
hallowed be your name.
Let your kingdom come;
Let your will be done on earth
as it is in heaven.
Give us today our daily bread
and forgive us our sins
as we forgive those
who sin against us.
Lead us not into temptation
but deliver us from evil.
For the kingdom, the power
and the glory are yours
for ever and ever.   Amen.

APPENDIX

1.

King David   Hello, Nathan. I've been thinking.

Nathan   Not too hard, I hope, your majesty.

King David   I would like to build a fantastic temple for God to live in. The best temple ever for the best and only God. We all have nice houses to live in, but the ark of the Covenant is still in a tent.

Nathan   Well, it sounds a very good idea, your majesty. Let me go and sleep on it and pray about it. See you tomorrow. Goodbye.

Narrator   So Nathan went away and next day he was back.

King David   Good morning, Nathan! What did God think of my idea?

Nathan   Well, it's a good idea and God is happy that you love him and worship him. But he is quite happy living in a tent and moving around with all of you. The temple can be built later on.

King David   Who will build it then?

Nathan   The temple will be built by your son, when he is king. But God has an important message for you.

King David   Really? What does he say?

Nathan   God wants you to know that he has planned a kingdom which will last for ever and ever. The king who will reign for ever will be from your own family. Long after your days are over, this King will bring joy to the whole world.

King David   Goodness, that's amazing. Excuse me, Nathan, I must go and say thank you to God for this.

Narrator   Hundreds of years later a woman was visited by an angel. The angel, whose name was Gabriel, told her she would have a rather special baby, and must call him Jesus, which means someone who saves or rescues.

2.

Gabriel   You are to call the child Jesus. He will be great and will be called the Son of the Most High. The Lord God will give him the throne of his father David, and he will reign over the house of Jacob for ever; his kingdom will never end.

(King David walks into the scene and says to the children sitting watching . . .)

King David   Hey, did you hear that? This woman is going to have the king that God promised would come! And this woman is engaged to Joseph, and he's from my family. So God was right. As usual. He's never lets you down, you know!

Gabriel   *(To King David)* Excuse me, but could I get on with my message to Mary, please?

King David   Oh, sure! Sorry to push into another time zone. I just got excited, that's all!

Mary   I am the Lord's servant. May it be to me as you have said.

Holy, most holy, all holy the Lord
(Sunday before Lent)

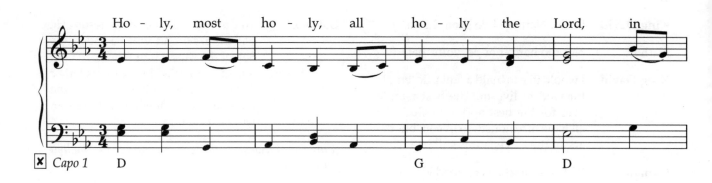

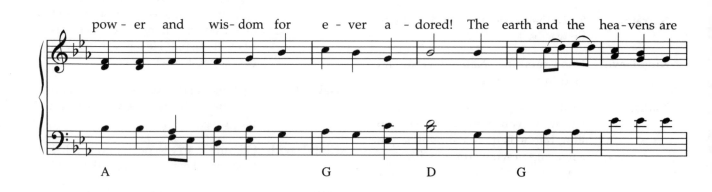

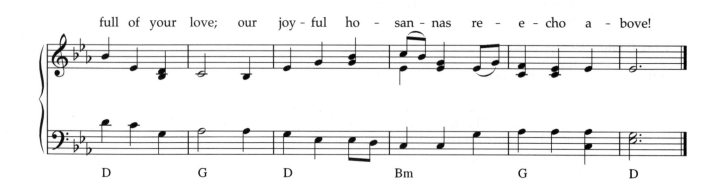

Words: Michael Forster. Music: traditional Irish melody, arr. Alan Ridout
Text and this arrangement © Copyright 1995 Kevin Mayhew Ltd

(Jesus walks into the room and the young man runs up to him, kneeling before him.)

Young man Good Teacher, what must I do to get eternal life?

(Jesus looks thoughtful, looks at the man, and helps him up.)

Jesus Why are you calling me good?

(Young man looks puzzled.)

Jesus No one is good, only God. You know the commandments? *(Young man nods, pleased, and counts them on his fingers as Jesus says them.)* Don't murder, don't commit adultery, don't steal, don't lie, don't cheat . . . *(The man looks puzzled again as this isn't one of the commandments.)* honour your father and mother . . .

Young man Yes, teacher, I know all that. I've been keeping the commandments since I was a little boy! But I still feel I'm missing out somewhere. It's more than just obeying the rules, isn't it?

(Jesus looks at him and smiles, placing his hands on the young man's shoulders.)

Jesus Yes, you're right, my son, there is more. There's something else you need to do – but it won't be easy for you. *(The young man looks pleased and ready to do anything. Jesus stands back and looks at him very seriously.)* Go and sell whatever you own and give it to the poor. All the treasure you have then will be treasure in heaven. Oh and then . . . *(Jesus smiles)* come and follow me!

Young man *(Half to himself)* Sell everything . . . EVERYTHING! Oh my goodness. *(His face clouds over and he looks at Jesus, shaking his head in disbelief before walking away, muttering to himself.)*

(Jesus walks towards the Rocks group, shaking his head sadly.)

Jesus Oh dear, he's so attached to all the things he owns, you see. Do you realise how difficult it is to enter God's kingdom? Especially if you're used to having lots of nice things around you. I reckon it's easier for a camel to get through the eye of a needle than for the rich to get into God's kingdom.

(Now you walk up to Jesus.)

You Goodness, Jesus, in that case who has any chance at all of entering the kingdom of God?

Jesus *(Shrugs)* Well, if you're talking about getting into God's kingdom all by yourself, I'd say no one has any chance at all! *(He smiles)* But if you let God do it in you – that's a very different matter. The impossible becomes possible!

You But some people give up everything to follow you, Jesus.

Jesus *(Nods)* That's right. And I can assure you that no one who sacrifices house, family or friends or land because of me will ever lose out. They'll get it all back many times over, in a different way, with eternal life thrown in!